LIVING HOLINESS

Helen Roseveare

BETHANY HOUSE PUBLISHERS
MINNEAPOLIS, MINNESOTA 55438
A Division of Bethany Fellowship, Inc.

Living Holiness was originally published in Great Britain by Hodder and Stoughton Limited, Mill Road, Dunton Green, Sevenoaks, Kent, England.

Published by Bethany House Publishers
A Division of Bethany Fellowship, Inc.
6820 Auto Club Road, Minneapolis, Minnesota 55438

Printed in the United States of America

Library of Congress Cataloging-in-Publication Data

Roseveare, Helen
   Living holiness

   Bibliography: p.
   1. Holiness.   2. Roseveare, Helen.   I. Title.
BT767.R67   1987   248.4   86-30781
ISBN 0-87123-952-3 (pbk.)

Contents

"Consider Him," let Christ thy pattern be
And know that He hath apprehended thee
To share His very life, His power divine,
And in the likeness of thy Lord to shine.

"Consider Him," so shalt thou, day by day,
Seek out the lowliest place and therein stay,
Content to pass away, a thing of nought,
That glory to the Father's name be brought.

Shrink not, O child of God, but fearless go
Down into death with Jesus: thou shalt know
The power of an endless life begin
With glorious liberty from self and sin.

"Consider Him," and thus thy life shall be
Filled with self-sacrifice and purity:
God will work out in thee the pattern true
And Christ's example ever keep in view.

"Consider Him," thy great High-Priest above
Is interceding in untiring love,
And He would have thee thus within the veil
By Spirit-breathed petitions to prevail.

"Consider Him," and as you run the race
Keep ever upward looking in His face:
And thus transformed, illumined thou shalt be,
And Christ's own image shall be seen in thee.

E. May Grimes (SAGM)
The Keswick Hymn Book (MMS)

Prologue

Holiness, without which no man shall see the Lord (Heb. 12:14) (AV).

The text which heads this page opens up a subject of deep importance. That subject is practical Holiness. It suggests a question which demands the attention of all professing Christians: are we holy? Shall we see the Lord?

Holiness by J. C. Ryle[1].

Prologue

"Doctor, can you come quickly? Timothy is bad."

There was an edge of fear in Mangadima's voice that Tuesday evening which warned me that three-year-old Timothy, Pastor Ambisayo's son, must be seriously ill.

* * *

The scene is a small clearing in the north-eastern border of the mighty Ituri rain forest in Central Africa, just a couple of degrees north of the equator. The time, July 1962. Rain, sunshine and a steamy humidity make up the climate: root vegetables and green leaves, soaked in palm oil, make up the diet. The normal additions of rice, peanuts and corn are sadly lacking as the rains came too late this year for the annual crops. Poverty – shattering, unbelievable poverty – is the lot of everyone. It is hard work to eke out an existence. Suffering has abounded over centuries. Axe-wounds fester; colds develop into pneumonia; women die in childbirth; children die before they learn to walk. Yet the people are surprisingly happy, accepting with stoical resignation that life must include daily hardship.

Here in this small, almost unknown village, a hospital has grown up. Wards and clinics are still mostly mud and thatch structures, though here and there permanent buildings of brick and cement are appearing, one or two even with corrugated roofing. There is no electricity. Water is gathered in disused two-hundred-litre petrol drums, as it pours off the roofing during daily downpours. The medical staff seek to serve the surrounding population of almost half a million people living in thousands of scattered villages within a radius of five hundred miles. The operative word is "serve". There is so little they can do with their extremely limited resources, compared to the work carried out in a modern, well-equipped hospital in the affluent industrialised world. But they can, and day after long day do, offer loving service with good nursing care.

A mile-long village borders the dirt-track road that runs from Isiro, the Government township fifty miles to the north, to Ibambi, the small commercial centre ten miles to the south. At the southern end of this village, two rows of small homes face each other across a sun-baked courtyard, housing both the forty male "medical" students during their two years of study and the families of the fifteen workmen. Between the workmen's quarters and the hospital quadrangle lies the square of "rooms" where families and friends of hospital patients can stay, to cook the meals and wash the clothes and bandages of their sick relatives. The hospital itself consists of a motley collection of permanent brick and very impermanent mud wards, a room for surgical operations and a large, open, covered area for the outpatients' clinics.

The doctor's home, which backs on to the hospital compound, is the focal point of all the community's activities, looking out, as it does, on the village square, with its small church to the right and the primary school classrooms to the left. Towards the northern end of the clearing lies the maternity complex, a pleasant brick building with ward and delivery rooms, and several small homes for the twelve pupils and staff midwives. Lastly, there is the home of the two European nurses. Flanking all are the well-kept food gardens amidst attractive sloping grass lands, bright with frangipani and poinsettias, the whole surrounded by the eternal forest.

The whole village throbs with life and activity. There is constant coming and going. Patients arrive at all hours, some from great distances, some walking, some being carried in makeshift stretchers, always accompanied by members of their families. Young men come, from near and far, to be trained as "medical auxiliaries". Yet, at the heart of the village, there is a close-knit family of nationals and missionaries to all of whom this village is home. The scene looks peaceful enough. Though to an outsider it may appear a little run-down and haphazard, to the team, whose very life blood has gone into its creation, it is a continuing source of wonder.

As for me, the doctor, Nebobongo *is* my life. Day and night, for more than seven years, I have sought to be available – to patients needing medical care; to students needing training; to workmen needing encouragement; above all, to the Church, the centre of the life of the village, in its worship and its teaching.

* * *

Mangadima's sudden urgent summons for help, just as dusk was falling at the end of another busy day, brought a premonition of trouble ahead. Pulling on my white coat, stuffing my stethoscope in its pocket, I picked up a storm lantern and accompanied Mangadima across the courtyard to the hospital village. Three weeks earlier, Timothy's mother had come to us with a badly fractured ankle. After ten days in the hospital, she had been moved to a room in the "square", as her bed in the ward was needed. We could watch her progress here, until she was well enough to walk the fifty miles back to her village of Babeyru, high in the gold mine mountain range to the south of Nebobongo. Her evangelist husband, Ambisayo, had joined her the previous weekend. He would probably stay with her about ten days, and preach in our church the next Sunday.

We stooped to enter the low doorway, and paused while our eyes grew accustomed to the darkness. Young Timothy was tossing and turning in his mother's arms, as she sought to comfort him. His breathing was laboured and rasping, his eyes wide open, fixed on space, unseeing and almost unblinking. He was hot, very hot. His arms seemed to twist in small convulsive jerks. I tried to listen to his chest but irritably he grabbed the stethoscope and pushed me away.

One thing was obvious. He was a very ill child.

We backed out of the room, and I asked Mangadima to help them to move into the spare room in my house, where I could more easily keep an eye on the lad through the night.

I hurried home to make the room ready for them, moving two tea-chests of bandages and hospital supplies into my own bedroom, and putting up a cot for Timothy.

His temperature had risen over the past three days, with no sign of the remissions typical of malaria. He had no apparent neck rigidity to indicate meningitis. As far as I could tell, his chest was clear of any tell-tale signs of pneumonia, though his throat was minimally inflamed. During that first night in my home, he became steadily more toxic, the restless agitation and fretful crying giving way to a listless apathy and muted whimpering. His eyes became glazed. His temperature soared. As I sponged the feverish body yet again, in the early light of the next morning, I noticed small blisters around his wrists and, without further inspection, subconsciously registered "scabies", the almost inevitable infestation of so many of Africa's village children.

I coaxed him to take a sip of water, but he dribbled it back, apparently unable to swallow. I considered inserting a stomach-tube that I might feed him more satisfactorily. Sponging him again with cool water, I saw blisters also on his legs.

The morning wore on. After doing the hospital ward round, I cancelled the students' lecture and returned to Timothy. His temperature was half a degree higher. Between the twisting heaves that accompanied each rasping breath, he lay still. Again I sponged him. There were blisters up his arms ... on his chest ... "Chickenpox," I thought automatically. Half of the children in our primary school had it just then. "One more thing that Timothy could have done without," I muttered to myself.

Suddenly, I realised.

I looked quickly, carefully, at the blisters. They had started at wrists and ankles, and spread inwards to the chest, rather than in the opposite direction as is usual in chickenpox. Yes, each blister showed the tell-tale central dimple. Timothy had smallpox.

Something inside me stood still. For a long silent minute, the world seemed to stop.

Smallpox!

A word of horror. I'd never seen a case of smallpox, but my mind rushed into activity, trying to remember all I'd learned. Of our village family of five hundred people, practically none had been vaccinated, except the three Europeans. This could have devastating results.

"Tuesday – Monday – Sunday –."

Timothy had been living among them for three days. There would have been countless contacts, as he had accompanied his mother to the water source, to the cook house, to morning prayers in church, to the out-patients' clinic. In ten days from last Sunday – I counted feverishly . . .

"Next Wednesday – today week – we can expect the next cases."

"And then . . . ?" I shuddered. My imagination pictured the worst.

What could I do?

The next twenty-four hours were filled with non-stop activity. A plan was drawn up. A bamboo fence was erected all round my home to isolate us from the rest of the compound. As far as possible, I would care in my home for all those who contracted the dread disease. Elaine, one of my nursing colleagues, would be responsible for the hospital, pharmacy and male students, and Florence would look after the maternity and leprosy care centres and girl pupils, each working with the African teams of qualified staff.

The whole village was sealed off from the surrounding communities. Trees across all access roads carried large notices to the public of their need to "leave us alone". No one was to come into, or leave, the village until further notice. All meetings – church, schools, social – were cancelled, and people asked to keep to their own family unit and not to visit one another. Congregating at the water source and in the cookhouses was strongly discouraged. Every effort was made to contain the infection, and to minimise the danger of a major outbreak.

A small quantity of smallpox vaccine was unearthed in the pharmacy supplies. Whether it was in or out of date, we dared not ask. Medical personnel and young Timothy's most likely contacts were vaccinated. Then what was left was used, as far as it would go, for the village and for the hospital "public".

Each day, I would "do a ward round" with the staff, from the back and front doors of my home, shouting across the twelve yards of no-man's land between house and fence, seeking to answer questions and advise on treatment for all the patients.

Timothy was worse, his right arm tight with swelling, his left arm an open running sore of coalesced vesicles. His breathing was increasingly difficult and I considered doing a tracheotomy. I fed him by tube, yet even so he was vomiting almost everything.

I sent two letters out of the village, carefully fumigated in my cookhouse oven over an open wood fire. One was to Government health authorities, notifying them of our situation: the other was to my mother in England, asking her to mobilise prayer on our behalf.

Timothy was slipping into a coma by Sunday morning.

Two women were moved into my home, both suspected to be developing smallpox, though neither had had close contact with Timothy during the previous week.

I was desperately tired – and afraid. What was going to happen? An epidemic could be catastrophic and wipe out my "family". I prayed earnestly and continuously that God would intervene on our behalf. There were no church services that Sunday, everyone praying in their own homes.

An imperceptible "waiting" filled the air. After lunch, wearily I glanced along my bookshelf for something to take my mind off the vast and heavy burden that had settled over us. There was a new book there, that I had received the previous Christmas from friends in England, *Holiness*, by Bishop J. C. Ryle. There was rarely time to read in the ordinary course of my busy life: but today was somewhat out of the ordinary!

I read the foreword by Dr Martyn Lloyd-Jones, and excitedly plunged into the introduction, before I was called out.

That afternoon, Timothy died.

I called our village pastor to the fence, using the small talking drum at my back door, and told him the sombre news. He and a team of workmen went in silence, through the drizzling rain, to dig a grave – a deep grave. As darkness fell that evening, they told me that all was ready, and, with sad hearts, leaving two spades leaning against the fence, they trudged slowly away into the dark.

An hour later, when all the villagers were indoors for the night, Timothy's father and I set out together, he carrying spades, storm lantern and other necessities, I carrying the stiffening body of the three-year-old. Together in the dark we lowered the body into the grave. Together, in silence except for the broken sobs of the father and the pattering of rain on the leaves, we shovelled earth into the grave. Together we stood with bowed heads, praying before we made our stumbling way back to my home. There we each changed and bathed, and then burned any garment that had touched the child, before we lay down, each burdened with our own thoughts, for the remaining hours of that night.

On the Monday the five of us settled down to live out the three weeks of quarantine in strict isolation. I read more of J. C. Ryle's book.

Tuesday morning, the two women who had joined us broke out in the typical smallpox rash. In the afternoon, yet another patient was sent over to us.

I sent an SOS to the African nursing team, six young men and two women. I was going to need an assistant. I could not cope with the day and night nursing, plus all the housework, cooking and laundry that would be involved in caring for this growing group. The assistant would have to be a volunteer. None of our staff had been previously vaccinated. Anyone joining me would be at the gravest risk of developing the killer disease.

Suzanne came. I wept – and welcomed her.

In the evening, she and I joined Pastor Ambisayo and his wife Batibama for a time of Bible reading and prayer. Picking up my Bible as we went along, I unwittingly picked up also Ryle's book on Holiness, as they lay together by my bed. After our time of fellowship, Suzanne went to the kitchen to make mugs of hot cocoa for us all, and I shared with Ambisayo a little of what I had read in the foreword and introduction to Bishop Ryle's book, translating one or two paragraphs into Swahili for him.

Suzanne brought the hot drinks.

As I stopped "reading", (translating aloud into Swahili as I read the English words), Ambisayo said, almost sharply, "Don't stop! God is speaking. These words are like honey." I read on, Suzanne and Batibama listening as intently as Ambisayo himself.

That evening set a pattern for each evening during the coming four and a half weeks, as our quarantine period eventually proved to be, for the following week two other women joined us, and then, a fortnight later, Suzanne herself developed the disease.

At that very point, the Lord stayed the epidemic. The six patients who had contracted the illness recovered completely. Meanwhile, vaccine had arrived from Government sources, and our medical team vaccinated over sixty thousand of the local population.

Each evening, as household chores were finished, meals prepared and served, medicines given out, cleaning and laundry done as needed, and each patient made as comfortable as possible, the four of us, Pastor Ambisayo and his wife Batibama, Suzanne and myself, gathered together and read our book on Holiness. Sometimes we continued late into the night, our hearts burning within us as we read the good words of "one of the greatest of Victorian evangelicals ... that man of granite, with the heart of a child"[2].

Ambisayo testified, at the end of our period of quarantine, that the reading of that book so changed his life that he could never be the same again. I know what he meant – I could echo his words. This book now is the direct result. If any reader, through my attempt to tackle the vast subject of Holiness, receives one fraction of the blessing that I received through reading J. C. Ryle's book over twenty years ago, all the effort in its preparation will have been amply rewarded. The story and setting of young Timothy's illness form the background to all that follows, for any growth in my life towards a *living* experience of Holiness began during my twenty years as a missionary in Zaire.

1

The start of the race

Therefore, let us run the race set before us. A race means ... concentration of purpose and will, strenuous and determined effort. It means that a man while he is on the course gives himself wholly to one thing – running with all his might. It means that for the time being he forgets everything for the all-absorbing desire – to gain the prize. The Christian course means this all through life: a whole-hearted surrender of oneself, to put aside everything for the sake of God and His favour. The men who enter the course are separated from the crowd of idle spectators: they each of them can say, One thing I do – they run.

Looking unto Jesus – there we have the inner life of the spirit, a heart always fixed on Jesus in faith and worship, drawing inspiration and strength from His example and His love.

The Holiest of All, by Andrew Murray[1].

1 The start of the race

It was a blistering hot Saturday afternoon, late in December.
The air shimmered above the dust-encrusted grass, under a
relentless blue sky. The palm trees stood erect yet listless, not
a ripple in their drooping fronds.

A crowd of excited young people filled the still air with
their chatter and laughter, and, as they ran hither and
thither, caused a red cloud to rise and hang over the field.
They were the only sign of life, as even the birds and cicadas
were silenced by the insufferable heat.

It was the annual sports day for the Nebobongo family!
Seventy to eighty orphan children from one to sixteen years
of age had been looking forward to this event for weeks.
Nearly one hundred other local children, mostly from the
village primary school, were beginning to arrive, with friends
and parents. The students from the medical auxiliary
training school and pupils from the assistant midwives
school had worked hard to prepare games and races,
jumping and hurdling, for every age group, to occupy the
next three hours; and workmen and their wives had prepared
a feast for everyone at the end of the day.

A whistle blew.

Remarkably, silence fell, and all eyes turned to the small
group of seniors gathered around a rickety camp-table at
one end of the field.

"We'll start," someone called out, "with a race for the six
and seven year olds, in first and second grade primary
school."

Eventually the children were sorted out, put in groups,
and arranged in line, with all the usual palaver of such an

undertaking, yet with minimal ill feeling and a lot of good-humoured laughter.

Everyone watched, called and encouraged the children. Perhaps the smaller ones began to see how a race was run, for a few minutes later their race was announced.

"All pre-schoolers now!"

What a mêlée resulted! What patience and tact were needed to sort them all out, get them into reasonably sized groups, and explain to them what they were to do – run thirty yards towards a white tape held across the far end of the course, carrying an orange perched on their curly black hair without touching it and without letting it fall off! At last they were ready to start. Pastor Ndugu was standing at the finishing line to pick out the winner.

"Just run to Pastor Ndugu!" everyone called out, frantically trying to head their youngsters in the right direction. The tiny mites, like a pack of puppies, ran hither and thither in every conceivable direction except the right one, most of them heading off delightedly to a relative or friend spotted in the crowd. No amount of cajoling or persuasion, shouting or demonstrating seemed to have any effect on them – that is, any of them except one.

Sturdy, four-year-old Mark trotted straight up the course, without looking to left or right, his orange firmly planted down into his curly mop, his eyes shining, paying no attention to all the other children, and completely undistracted by the shouts and laughter of the onlookers.

He ran straight through the white tape and into the arms of the waiting pastor!

The crowd cheered with delight, as they realised why just the one youngster had understood, and obeyed, and won the race by an enormous margin – the pastor was his grandfather!

* * *

Recently, while doing some further study, I had to write an essay on the moral attributes of God. When I began, I was fairly sure that God's one great over-riding attribute was *love*. "God is love." I believed that all other attributes flowed from that one central fact of the love of God. But as I studied, I began to realise that love, like all the other attributes of God, is part of the greatest attribute of all, the *Holiness* of God.

"God is holy."

This fact shines out of every page of the Scriptures, brilliant as the midday sun. It begins to blind one to all the other factors. Just as the sun's light is broken down by a raindrop into the separate colours of the spectrum, so the Holiness of God is broken down, so to speak, into the many-coloured spectrum of all His attributes – His goodness and mercy, His loving kindness and forbearance, His righteousness and justice, His truth and wrath – so that we can see and understand what makes up this Holiness.

Professor R. A. Finlayson, delivering the 1955 Dr G. Campbell Morgan Memorial Lecture at Westminster Chapel in London, used this same illustration as he summed up his definition of Holiness. "The sum of all God's attributes, the outshining of all that God is," said Finlayson, "is Holiness." He continued: "As the sun's rays, containing all the colours of the spectrum, come together in the sun's shining and blend into light, so all the attributes of God come together in His self-manifestation and blend into Holiness"[2].

For over forty years, the thought of the "Holiness of God" became an irresistible influence in my life, as the "goal" of my "race". The writer of the letter to the Hebrews expresses the course of our life as "the race marked out for us", for which we must "throw off everything that hinders and the sin that so easily entangles," and which we must "run with perseverance" (Heb. 12:1). As I thought and prayed, the great Holy God became for me the One who drew me constantly by His Love and through His Grace; just as the presence of Pastor Ndugu at the winning tape drew young Mark unerringly forward.

All my Christian life, I have had an ever-increasing desire

to know more, in practical experience, of what Holiness really means. If Isobel Kuhn had not used it already, the title of this book might well have been "By Searching". From the moment that I knew that Jesus Christ, God's Son, had died to save me, bearing the penalty and guilt of my sins, I became conscious of a need to search for Holiness, a way to *be* holy – not that I called the object of my search "Holiness"; rather, it was to be what I considered good, and to cease to be what I knew was bad.

No one told me that this longing in my heart was the work of the Holy Spirit and the beginning of what is called "sanctification" – the process of making me holy, like unto the Lord Jesus. In fact, no one told me that this sanctifying work of the Spirit in my heart was the essential proof that He had regenerated my life. As soon as one is justified and saved, the work of sanctification must begin, and it is the Holy Spirit Himself who causes one to "hunger after righteousness", to want to be good, as He makes real in one's heart that which God sees to be good; and to want to cease to be bad, as He shows one those things that displease God.

No. I did not understand that then; but I just knew, with a deep inner consciousness, that there must BE a goal to which my whole Christian life should be directed. Even though I hardly knew the word, let alone what it meant, I sensed that that goal was Holiness. So it came about that after the overwhelming joy of realising that my sins had been forgiven, I started out on a long quest after Holiness.

I thank God that the first gift I received after I was saved was a Bible: and the first teaching was an exhortation to read it daily. I was given a card with suggested portions of Scripture for consecutive reading, and told how to pray, read, meditate and then seek to put into practice anything that God said through His Word. The Bible became for me the guidebook to living, showing how "to run the race" that was set before me, as I strove towards this desired goal of Holiness – that is, Godliness – and sought, by His grace, to live a life that would be pleasing to the God who had created and redeemed me.

So I started out by studying the epistle to James, followed by Peter's letters.

"Make every effort to add to your faith goodness; and to goodness, knowledge; and to knowledge, self-control; and to self-control, perseverance; and to perseverance, godliness; and to godliness, brotherly kindness; and to brotherly kindness, love," said Peter, in 2 Peter 1:5-8. "For if you possess these qualities in increasing measure, they will keep you from being ineffective and unproductive in your knowledge of our Lord Jesus Christ."

I was already beginning to want, more than anything else, to grow in my knowledge of the Lord Jesus Christ.

Peter, I found, gave a further admonition: "Be all the more eager to make your calling and election sure. For if you do these things, you will never fall, and you will receive a rich welcome into the eternal kingdom of our Lord and Saviour Jesus Christ" (2 Pet. 1:10). That sounded like what I was after!

In that epistle, he continues to stress this aspect of our Christian life, and underlines the fact that we constantly need to "add to ..." if we are to grow. He stresses that, far from being negligent in doing this, we should remember his teaching, that we might be stirred up to even greater endeavour.

"Add to ..." That phrase kept coming back to me. It was a simple, straightforward thought. I was reasonably good at mathematics, and understood the basic concept of addition.

Then, two days later, I came to another phrase: "grow in the grace and knowledge of our Lord and Saviour Jesus Christ" (2 Pet. 3:18). Equally, I knew enough about biology to understand the concept of growth!

Addition and growth. Physical and biological. The two concepts, taking root in my heart within one month of becoming a Christian, were to be the first stepping stones in my search for Holiness. I spent all the time I could, mornings and evenings, studying the Bible, "soaking up", like the proverbial sponge, the Word of God. It excited me and challenged me, convinced me and stirred me. Every day I sought to "add to" my knowledge and understanding of God, and to "grow in" grace and in the outworking of Scriptural principles in daily conduct.

That is where the first crunch came. My head began to know answers, but my life was not consistent. I began to know where to find such texts as: "This is the victory that has overcome the world, even our faith" (1 John 5:4), but I knew that I was not living a victorious Christian life. I taught my Sunday School pupils about the call of Peter, and how he "left everything and followed" Jesus (Luke 5:1–11), yet I knew there were practices in my life, particularly in my thoughts, that I had not left behind. Oh, I wanted to follow Jesus. I was completely convinced mentally that nothing else would ever really satisfy me, except obedience to the Lord Jesus Christ, but the fact was not being worked out in my life.

The Bible clearly stated: "If anyone is in Christ, he is a new creation," and I knew it was true! I *was* new. My whole outlook and attitude to life were changed. My desires and ambitions were being completely re-directed. Yet the same verse went on "the old has gone, the new has come!" (2 Cor. 5:17), and this simply was *not* true in my experience. Obviously it should have been true, but some of the "old things" had not passed away, nor been replaced by new.

I went to meetings because I wanted to be challenged by great speakers to "renounce all", and to deny myself and to take up my cross daily and follow the Lord Jesus as we are told to do in Luke 9:23. I stayed behind for counselling. I re-dedicated myself. I feverishly searched in my heart to discover any deliberately unconfessed sin that might be hindering my going forward into the coveted life of sanctification. That, as I began to understand the terminology, was the process of being made holy, made to be actually more and more like the Lord Jesus in my daily life and activities.

I went to Keswick conventions to have time to be quiet in God's presence and to allow the Holy Spirit to melt my hard heart and reveal anything that was preventing my "acceptance by faith" of this deeper-life experience for which I longed. Yet each convention seemed only to bring me into a deeper consciousness of guilt and frustration.

I determined to "live as though I had what I sought, and then see what would happen", as some exhorted me to do. I taught in a Girl Crusaders' Union Bible Class each Sunday. I led ward services in the hospital where I was a student. I was known as a "keen Christian", outwardly saying and doing the correct things; yet inwardly I struggled with a sense of failure, of deception, almost of unbelief.

I went to live at the headquarters of the Worldwide Evangelization Crusade (as it was then called), and committed myself to a future life of missionary service in its ranks, still seeking by this means to "add to..." and to "grow in ...". Nevertheless, at the same time, my heart was unsatisfied. I was *not* "holy as He is holy". My endeavours to "sanctify myself" were spasmodic and moody, and usually ineffectual, although, by God's gracious mercy, the desire to be holy and to please Him continued to gnaw at my heart.

I joined a Pentecostal Assembly of God, and I thank God for the deep stirring of reality that swept through me. The infectious joy, the exuberant singing, the dynamic power in the open-air witnessing – all this was exciting and brought a new dimension to my Christian life. I began to enjoy going to their prayer meeting each week. Yet ... as the "novelty" wore off, as I became accustomed to the new songs and to the freer atmosphere and to the absence of inhibitions in worship and witness ... I realised that the deep inner longing after Holiness remained unabated and unassuaged. This "baptism in the Spirit" with joy in worship and with power for witness was not the sanctifying grace that I longed for. I knew that I was not more Christlike in my daily living.

Dr J. I. Packer, speaking of himself in the preface to J. C. Ryle's book on Holiness, says [that] all "he could do was repeatedly reconsecrate himself, scraping the inside of his psyche till it was bruised and sore, in order to track down still unyielded things by which the blessing was perhaps being blocked". I understand so well what he means!

Then I came to the next stepping stone: I heard Mrs Stanley Banks preach on Matthew 5:14-16. Christians were to be lanterns to carry Christ, the Light, into the world. As I remember, she illustrated her talk with a large storm lantern, which she filled with clean paraffin oil and then lit with a match. Holding the lantern aloft for us to see, the lights in the hall were turned out. But we could see nothing. Hardly a flicker of light could pass through the filth and grime on the lantern's glass. Oh, yes, the light was shining steadily inside, but it could not get out. While the glass remained dirt-encrusted, the lantern was virtually useless.

"Let your light shine before men, that they may see your good deeds and praise your Father in heaven" was her message. Keep the glass clean and shining, and the Light will stream through to those in darkness.

At this same time, God was graciously pouring out His power in mighty revival blessing on the Church in Ruanda. Missionaries came home on furlough and shared with us the "secret" of revival. African pastors came to England to tell us of the marvel of God's blessing, their faces radiant with joy. Each one told us of the need to keep short accounts with God, and to share with one another, as together they sought to "walk in the Light". This phrase summed up the three parts of their testimony: quick confession of sin as the Holy Spirit pricks the conscience to realise that wrong has been done or thought; seeking cleansing and forgiveness for that sin through the merits of Christ's death on Calvary; and owning up to it in the human fellowship, putting right what was wrong, as far as they were able.

Things began to fit into place: this was patently the method by which the glass of the lantern might be kept clean.

With these thoughts filling my mind, I sailed for the Belgian Congo (Zaire of today) and there attended a national Bible School for eighteen months, growing in the knowledge of the Word and seeking, with God's help, to cleanse my glass daily.

Mr Ted Hegre, principal of the Bethany Fellowship in Minneapolis, visited our Bible School and gave several talks to us. These talks became the next stepping stone in my search after practical Holiness. We were given three small booklets with clear, coloured diagrams to illustrate his teaching on the place of the Cross in the life of the believer[3]. He delineated for us the Scriptural principle, that Holiness is God's will for every Christian, reminding us of what Paul wrote to the Thessalonians: "It is God's will that you should be sanctified" (1 Thess. 4:3). This, he made clear, should be considered the immediate follow-up to becoming a Christian. It is almost like the name on the other side of the door: we enter the Christian life through the door marked Regeneration (to be born again) and find Sanctification (to be made holy) written on the other side. An unholy Christian life is a contradiction in terms. If one plants a peanut, he said, one expects a harvest of peanuts, not of corn! If Jesus Christ is born in our hearts, we should expect Christ-likeness to show in our lives.

Even more than Mr Hegre's teaching, what remained with us after his visit was his own Christ-likeness. He stayed in our home, and I saw him "off-duty" as well as on the platform. I drove him from place to place during his stay with us. Be it at the breakfast table, or at the roadside while we repaired a punctured tyre, or while preaching in church, he was consistently the same. It was all so obviously "for real". There was no pose; there were no pious platitudes.

Then there was the smallpox epidemic, at our small forest hospital in north-east Zaire, and the weeks of enforced quarantine, when we had the opportunity to read carefully and prayerfully J. C. Ryle's book, *Holiness*. That was the next stepping stone in my search. When I finished reading the book, Ambisayo breathed, "I shall never be the same again!" and this was not just because of the death of his little boy, but because he realised, as never before, the majestic purpose of God, who had called us "to live a holy life" (1 Thess. 4:7).

* * *

Since 1973, I have been living in the United Kingdom, and seeking to present the desperate need of the three thousand million people, alive today, who have never yet heard of our Lord Jesus Christ and of the redemption He wrought for them at Calvary. These are the "hidden peoples" in more than ten thousand ethnic groups around our world. As I try to present their needs, I pray earnestly that the Holy Spirit will stir hearts to make a response. It seems so obvious to me that Christian young people who come to these meetings should rise up and *go*, to tell forth the Gospel "to the uttermost parts of the world".

But so few do. Why is the response so poor? What is wrong?

Is it that we Christians today have an inadequate understanding of God's Holiness and therefore of His wrath against sin and of the awfulness of a Christless eternity? If we were gripped by the two facts – of the necessity for judgment of sin because God is holy; and of the necessity of Holiness in the Christian that he may represent such a God to others – would we not "hunger and thirst after righteousness" whatever the cost, and would not others then see Christ in us, and be drawn to Him?

In other words, if we were to rightly present the Scriptural teaching on the need of Holiness in the life of every believer, we should not need to plead for missionaries. Would the former not result in the latter?

So I found myself not now searching after Holiness for myself only, but rather seeking how to present this wonderful facet of Christian doctrine to others, that true missionary fervour might be stirred up in us all.

If we have begun to appreciate the awful sinfulness of sin, and that the only way a holy God could save us from its guilt and penalty was by the death – the actual, physical, brutal death – of His only Son, we would realise *from what* He had redeemed us. Understanding this, would we not then understand *for what* He had redeemed us – for unremitting service, as His ambassadors, telling others, while it is yet the day of grace, of the wonderful news of Christ's death for sinners?

If we are to fulfil this purpose for which we are saved, not only must the emphasis be on the *fact* of Holiness as seen in Christ, but also on the essential *need* of Holiness in our lives that we may properly reveal Christ to others.

A testimony to salvation without a resultant Holiness of character and conduct is a contradiction. It is, as St James says, a dead faith, if it has not the witness of works.

With all my heart I endorse the fact that we are not, and never can be, saved by good works; we are saved and redeemed because Christ died on the Cross of Calvary in our place, becoming our sin, our great Substitute:

> Bearing scorn and scoffing rude,
> In my place condemned He stood.

We are saved as the result of Redemption, wrought for us by our Saviour alone. We are no longer our own. We have been bought at a price, the price of His shed blood. We are now His, our bodies indwelt by the risen Saviour through the ministry of the Holy Spirit. He, working in us and through us, will do the "yet greater works" that He promised, and our faith, which has brought us to know and acknowledge our Redeemer, will reveal itself alive and active by the fruit that is seen in our character, and the acts that transform our conduct.

"By their fruit you will recognise them" (Matt. 7:20).

* * *

If we needed any further incentive to stir us to holy living, surely it would be in the certain hope of Christ's return, and a longing in our hearts to be found watching and waiting to welcome Him.

But the Day of the Lord will come like a thief, [Peter says

in 2 Peter 3:10–12]. The heavens will disappear with a roar; the elements will be destroyed by fire, and the earth and everything in it will be laid bare.

Since everything will be destroyed in this way, what kind of people ought you to be? You ought to live holy and godly lives as you look forward to the Day of God and speed its coming.

Listen also to the words of the apostle John, in his letter to the scattered Christians of his day, many of whom were already suffering persecution under the Roman empire: "continue in Him, so that when He appears we may be confident and unashamed before Him at His coming" (1 John 2:28).

Everyone who knows that he is born again and has this glorious hope of meeting the Saviour unashamedly when He returns, will seek to purify himself, John goes on to say in 1 John 3:1–3. This "indispensable necessity of holy living" as John Stott expresses it in his commentary on the apostle's letter, is not only that we be ready to greet Christ when He returns in glory to reign triumphantly, but also that we be ready to fulfil the very purpose of Christ's first coming, to "take away our sins" and to "destroy the works of the devil"[4].

The apostle John is very clear about the essential characteristic of a Christian: "no one who lives in Christ keeps on sinning," and again: "no one who is born of God will continue to sin (habitually)." He is not saying that it is impossible for a Christian to sin. What he is saying is that it is impossible for a Christian both to abide in Christ and to continue in habitual, deliberate sin. The heretics of his day either presumed a blindness to sin, saying it was not there, or were merely indifferent to it, saying that it did not matter. These are still the devil's tactics, as he endeavours to blind our eyes to the total incongruity of "continuing in sin" once we have been redeemed by the precious blood of Christ.

Paul also speaks of the hope of Christ's return as an

incentive to holy living. In Titus 2:11–14, he makes the statement:

> For the grace of God that brings salvation has appeared to all men.
> It teaches us to say "No" to ungodliness and worldly passions,
> And to live self-controlled, upright and godly lives in this present age,
> While we wait for the blessed hope – the glorious appearing of our great God and Saviour, Jesus Christ,
> Who gave Himself for us to redeem us from all wickedness and to purify for Himself a people that are His very own, eager to do what is good.

Yes, as we look for that "blessed hope", the urge to be holy will fill our hearts, for, as the writer to the Hebrews says: "Without Holiness no one will see the Lord" (Heb. 12:14). This echoes Christ's own words in His Sermon on the Mount: "Blessed are the pure in heart, for they will see God" (Matt. 5:8).

* * *

My longing to be pleasing to God in my daily living has continued, not so much now as a search after a state of existence called "Holiness" to be obtained by faith, or by "letting go and letting God", or by deeper degrees of consecration, but rather by a deliberate acknowledgment of certain steps that must be taken daily in the "running of the race marked out for us".

These "steps" are the orderly working of the Holy Spirit in our lives to achieve the God-given goal and to bring us to Christian maturity. According to our degree of stubbornness and unresponsiveness, this purpose of the Holy Spirit may need many years, indeed a lifetime, for its fulfilment.

During times of revival, however, it appears that this

spiritual activity has often been speeded up, to bring about the same "living Holiness" in a believer, possibly in the course of a month or two. By studying the Spirit's work during such revivals, I came to recognise these "steps" in a progression towards the realisation of "living Holiness".

As I have read through many wonderful and exciting accounts of revival outbreaks in the Christian Church during the past one hundred and fifty years, a certain pattern *has* emerged clearly.

On each occasion, the Holy Spirit started His work in the heart of someone by convicting him of sin, leading him to godly repentance and, as far as was possible, to restitution. As each forgiven and restored sinner came to realise something more of what Christ had done for him at Calvary, the love of God flooded over him, filling his heart with a desire to know God's Word and to search out His commands, that he might obey them. By the grace of God, this way of obedience developed in the believer a truly Christlike desire to serve others. "The Son of Man did not come to be served, but to serve, and to give His life as a ransom for many" (Matt. 20:28).

When Christ washed the disciples' feet in the upper room, the evening before He was crucified, He told them to serve one another as He had served them.

When He offered the special morsel to Judas Iscariot at their last supper together, loving him even when He knew that He was about to be betrayed by him, our Lord told the other disciples to love one another as He had loved them.

The Holy Spirit desires to work in me the grace of repentance, purifying and cleansing me as I deliberately mortify and put away sinful practices.

He then pours into my heart the love of God, causing me to be able to love God truly and sincerely, with no ulterior motives, no subtle self-pleasing or self-gratification.

This love will reveal itself by an ever-increasing desire to obey God in every smallest detail, as the Holy Spirit prompts me through the reading of the Scriptures.

And this obedience will result in untiring service to my fellow men, to the glory of God, untarnished by any thought of what I personally will "get out of it".

This is the ministry of the Holy Spirit to bring about "living Holiness" in the life of every Christian believer.

One way, then, to enter into a living experience of Holiness is, surely, to follow these four defined steps, continuously asking the Holy Spirit to work in us a true hatred of sin, to fill us to overflowing with a great love for God, to set our wills to obey Him fully as a demonstration of that love, and to serve one another as an outworking of that obedience.

2

First step – Repentance

The carnal mind is enmity against God (Rom. 8:7) (AV).

SIN IS ENMITY. The word "enmity" toward God suggests more than the hostility that enemies have toward one another. Enmity is the personification of all hostility. Enemies may be reconciled, but enmity never is reconciled. Indeed, the only way to reconcile enemies is to destroy enmity.

Sin is ENMITY TOWARD GOD. Not only is it enmity itself, but it is "enmity against God". Indeed, it has chosen to have God Himself as its almighty enemy. Although it opposes the work of grace in us, its nature and purpose above all is to oppose God. Sin attacks Holiness and God's authority in our lives. It hates the yoke of the Lord.

John Owen[1].

2 First step – Repentance

"How clean do my hands have to be, to be clean?"

* * *

The compound was strangely still, a great quietness brooding over the village. Only the air trembled in the heat, lifting a veil of fine red dust that shimmered over all it touched. The very birds were motionless and silent as, in the scorching midday, the sun stared down relentlessly upon the baked courtyard. No one stirred. Even the leaves were too tired to rustle.

Suddenly, the silence was shattered. A bell clanged, startling the air and birds alike: but its clarion call was completely submerged by the tumult of over one hundred primary school children, let loose into the courtyard for their noon recess by four exhausted school masters.

Hot? Who cared?

Dusty? What of it?

Tired? Only of school!

There seemed to be one thousand rather than one hundred children around. They were everywhere – laughing, shouting, jumping, running – no one still, no one quiet. A group on one side were leap-frogging energetically over each other's bent backs; two little girls to the left were vigorously turning a skipping rope while others ran in and out, dodging the falling line. Some lads were shinning up the kimo-mango tree, shaking down the ripe (if forbidden) fruit to a hungry crowd below. Others were boisterously playing touch-and-run between the coffee bushes. The clouds of red dust rose higher and higher into the dazzling blue sky. Pandemonium reigned!

Yet as quickly as the crowd of children had erupted, it was gone, all surging in one direction as though drawn by a giant magnet. Down to the water-holes. Down the steep, rough pathway, winding between thick undergrowth, jumping over fallen tree-trunks, dodging round obstructing ant-hills, slipping down the last ten slithery yards into the cool water below the spring. Their laughter and shouts echoed to and fro among the giant trees, as they swung on the vast lianas and splashed in the shallow pool. Brilliant-coloured kingfishers darted off into the surrounding forest to the protection of the dark silence.

A distant drum throbbed.

Surely its sound could never penetrate the babbling noise of the army of happy children? Yet, as one man, they set off helter-skelter, tugging each other and clawing at over-hanging branches, clambering up the slippery slope, up the grassy pathway, up, up ... back into the sunlight. A dash across the courtyard brought them breathless to line up for "kula chakula" – the day's meal. Jostling and nudging, with only the vaguest attempt at silence, they looked eagerly at the full plates on the trestle tables. Then one of them spied Mama Malata (one of the devoted widows who cared for this noisy, healthy, happy bunch of Africa's orphan children) coming with a large tureen and ladle.

"Ni supo ya karanga leo!"

And the whole crowd burst into excited clapping. Peanut soup was being poured over each heaped plate of sombi leaves and roasted plantains. This was a special luxury that did not often brighten the usually drab diet.

"Kimya!"

The voice of authority drowned the hundred chattering tongues, and with one word of command imposed an impressive silent attention. One hundred heads bowed, hands folded, as together they thanked God for the meal that had once again been provided.

Pressing forward, the clumsy line filed past Authority, each child showing the palms of his or her hands as they went.

"Jaki, go and wash your hands!"

Those who had already passed inspection paid no attention, hurrying to a place at a table, laughing and chatting again.

Those still in the queue leant forward to see Jaki, the hapless victim, some grinning with mischievous glee that it wasn't them, others quietly sympathetic.

"But, Miss, I have washed them!"

"Jaki, look at them – they're filthy!"

"Please, Miss, I *did* wash them! I did, I truly did."

"Miss, he did. I saw him, down at the pool," shouted a friend.

Authority was unimpressed.

"Jaki, just look at your hands. Are they clean?"

"But I washed – I washed. I really washed!" wailed the culprit.

"I merely asked you to *look* at your hands, and tell me if *you* think they are clean," was the patient rejoinder of Authority.

As he turned to leave the queue and make his lonely way back to the water-hole, the luckless lad could be heard muttering, "But how clean do my hands have to be, to be clean?"

A good question, and perhaps not as ludicrous as might appear on first reading. Some of us have asked a similar question, perhaps, in very different circumstances and yet with the same desperation at having failed again.

"How holy do I have to be, to be holy?"

How hard it is to conceive of the possibility of "being holy" when daily we are conscious of failure! Jaki had probably dabbled his hands in the cool water, and in the dim half-light down at the pool, surrounded by the mighty forest, maybe they did look clean – at least, cleaner than they had been previously. When he had clambered back up to the courtyard and into the brilliance of midday sunshine, they

just did not look clean any longer. Listen to the words of the
Psalmist:

> Who may ascend the hill of the Lord?
> Who may stand in His holy place?
> He who has clean hands and a pure heart,
> Who does not lift up his soul to an idol
> Or swear by what is false (Ps. 24:3,4).

We all know that the nearer we seek to walk to our
Saviour, the more conscious we are of the "dirt". The
brilliant purity of Christ's Holiness shows up the shoddy
impurity of our daily lives, just as the sun reveals the dirt that
the shadows have hidden.

Jaki had to be convinced that his hands *were* dirty. Then
he should have been sorry that this was so, and in
consequence, put the matter right. Unfortunately, he was
unconvinced, and his obedience was a forced one, simply
given that he might be allowed to enjoy his midday meal. If
he determined not to be caught again with dirty hands, it was
certainly not because of a hatred of dirt!

We, in like manner, have to be convinced of sin in our
lives, and that this sin is "dirt" in the eyes of a holy God,
whose "eyes are too pure to look on evil", and who "cannot
tolerate wrong" (Hab. 1:13). This conviction of sin should
lead us to repentance and true sorrow for that which grieves
God; a godly repentance which, in turn, should lead us to a
deliberate intention to forsake the sin and be done with it, to
turn "*from* idols *to* ... God" (1 Thess. 1:9).

Sadly, one has to acknowledge that, just as Jaki went to
wash his hands in order to be allowed to have his meal, so we
can confess and make restitution for our sin in order to "feel
good", with no heart involvement and no realisation that our
sin has grieved the heart of the God who loves us.

Jesus wants His children to show true repentance. His first
message was: "Repent, for the kingdom of heaven is near"
(Matt. 4:17), and one of His final instructions to His

disciples before His ascension was that they should preach "repentance and forgiveness of sins ... in His Name" (Luke 24:47) everywhere, to all men.

What exactly is this that we call sin? Certainly only as we come to an understanding of what sin is, of how sinful sin is, and the price that has to be paid to eradicate it, can we hope to enter into an understanding of Holiness. J. C. Ryle defines sin as follows:

A sin consists in doing, saying, thinking or imagining, anything that is not in perfect conformity with the mind and law of God. Sin is the transgression of the law. The slightest outward or inward departure from absolute mathematical parallelism with God's revealed will and character constitutes a sin, and at once makes us guilty in God's sight[2].

Maybe it would be helpful to us to accompany Jeremiah on his visit to the house of the potter. Do you remember the story, recorded in Jeremiah 18:1–6? Two or three thousand years ago, God sent Jeremiah to watch the potter at work, creating a vessel on his wheel, in order that He might teach the prophet how He wished to work on the lives of His people:

This is the word that came to Jeremiah from the Lord: "Go down to the potter's house, and there I will give you My message."

So I went down to the potter's house, and I saw him working at the wheel. But the pot he was shaping from the clay was marred in his hands; so the potter formed it into another pot, shaping it as seemed best to him.

Then the word of the Lord came to me: "O house of Israel, can I not do with you as this potter does?" declares the Lord. "Like clay in the hand of the potter, so are you in My hand, O house of Israel."

* * *

One overcast day, during the rainy season, I accompanied the womenfolk of our village on an annual excursion. The peanuts had been harvested, and the rice crop planted. There was no immediate work waiting to be done in the fields. The children were in school, and the menfolk busy repairing the brick kiln. We set off shortly after sun-up, before the heat of the day began in earnest, carrying our rough hoes over our shoulders and small packs of smoked plantains, securely wrapped in banana leaves, fixed in the cloth bands around our waists.

Singing, we made our way for a short distance along the pot-holed highway, and then turned off, eastwards, down a winding forest track between mighty redwoods. Orchids grew here and there among the lush undergrowth, pale and colourless in the absence of daylight, since this was practically obliterated by the thick canopy of foliage forty feet above them. Small white butterflies darted in and out of the flickering shadows, alighting momentarily on damp piles of animal droppings, their wings held erect for instant flight as our footsteps disturbed them.

Skirting a six-foot high, granite-hard ant-hill; clambering over a fallen tree and the mass of ferns that grew out of its rotting heart; slithering down a muddy bank and through the stagnant waters between tall marsh grasses; scrambling up again, holding on to the long, trailing lianas until we could get grips of firmer branches – we made our way through the endless gloom of the green jungle, accompanied by the sharp jeering of monkeys swinging high above us and the shrieks of disturbed parrots. At last, we reached a small sluggish stream, our chosen destination, where the women knew they could find the proper clay essential for the making of their earthen jars.

Clothes tucked into their waist bands, the women stood in the stream and dug down into its bed with their hoes, churning up the water into a muddy pool. Hoes thrown down on the bank, they bent lower and worked with their hands to dislodge chunks of the thick, pale clay. Staggering out of the stream, they laid the clay on the grass to drain, while more was unearthed. It was hot, and the work heavy, and the air full of midges. Sweat poured off their bodies as they heaved the sodden clay from stream bed to bank. After two or three hours, the women judging that they had all they could carry, legs and arms were scraped and sluiced in the muddy waters, and rubbed with banana leaves to get off the worst of the clinging clay. We scattered to collect leaves in which to roll the heavy chunks, lianas with which to tie the bundles together, and branches on which to sling them to carry them home.

This journey home seemed longer, and somehow lacked the stimulus of the morning trek, as we trudged, laden and weary, the five or six miles back to the village, arriving as the sun was low in the west. The small fires behind each home were already crackling into life for the preparation of the evening meals.

Next day we carried our burdens down towards the water-hole, to bury the clay in the damp soil, where it would lie to "mature" until the dry season made it possible for us to leave the field work to make the earthen vessels needed for the following year.

As Christmas approached, with the rice harvest having been gathered in successfully and cotton sown in all the available land, the rains ceased and the earth began to crack as it dried in the searing sun and easterly winds. The time was now ripe to retrieve the clay and start the annual task of moulding and baking the various vessels for water, cooking, storing palmfat and rice. Each woman kneaded her lump methodically, as dough for bread, feeling for and pinching out all the small stones and pebbles that it contained, and squeezed the clay into a smooth, sticky paste. It was rolled, folded, pounded again and again, until all the grit and gravel was eliminated. Eventually it looked like long sausages of malleable putty.

The women, sitting on their heels, or squatting on their low, three-legged stools, chatting nonchalantly among themselves, made the work look easy. Carefully, they moulded each "sausage" between the right fingers and thumb, while turning the growing vessel with the left hand. Deftly, the thinning clay was pressed into a finer and finer ribbon-band, and worked around the jar above the previous band – round and round, shaping each contour to an exact symmetry. As the jar grew, a speck of dust, less than a pinhead in size, or a variation of less than a hair's breadth in the even thickness of the ribbon, though invisible to a casual onlooker, would cause the women to unwind the band, re-mould the clay, and re-do the work, striving after perfection with an indescribable patience.

Their meticulous care and standard of absolute accuracy, true to some preconceived pattern, was fascinating to watch – all to make a vessel for everyday household use, that would only last at most a year, and cost at most a few pence in the market.

> Yet, O Lord, You are our Father.
> We are the clay, You are the Potter;
> we are all the work of Your hand (Isa. 64:8).

> Know that the Lord is God.
> It is He who made us, and we are His (Ps. 100:3).

For we are God's workmanship, created in Christ Jesus to do good works, which God prepared in advance for us to do (Eph. 2:10).

As we see God as the Potter and ourselves as the clay in His hands to be moulded into the pattern that He has already planned, ready for the job He has purposed, it is easy to understand that the grit or gravel represents the sin in our lives that spoils the design. The finer the walls of the clay vessel become, the more clearly will a speck of grit be seen.

Godly repentance is the willingness to allow the Master Potter to extrude that grit. It is the birth of the desire to turn away from all that is not holy, and must be the first step towards Holiness.

God cannot allow sin to remain in the lives of His children. The "vase" He is making would be marred, and that is inconceivable. No, indeed! Sin must be cast out, and for this God must work into the heart of each believer a realisation of the sinfulness of sin, from which it cost the very Son of God His life-blood to redeem us. In turn, as we realise the sinfulness of sin, the Holy Spirit can give us a growing hatred for that sin which crucified the Saviour.

We cannot bring this about ourselves. Human nature only hates the consequences of sin, the punishment that society decrees when sin is exposed. We hardly even consider sin as sin, until we are "caught out". If we can "get away with it" we are relieved, we forget it, cover it up and carry on, doubtless to sin again and repeat the process. Only God the Holy Spirit can plant real hatred of sin in the human heart.

* * *

In July 1953, we had the privilege of being part of an extraordinary work of the Holy Spirit, when we watched God planting this hatred of sin in the hearts of church members at Ibambi, in what was then the Belgian Congo. We clearly saw the Master Potter at work, fashioning His vessels.

Forty-five years earlier, in 1908, C. T. Studd, already fifty years old and with his body ravaged by sickness, had been arrested by the ambiguous wording of a public notice, "Cannibals want missionaries!" advertising a meeting to be addressed by the great explorer of Africa, Dr Karl Kumm.

"In the middle of the continent," wrote C. T. Studd later, "Dr Kumm said there were numbers of tribes who had never heard the story of Jesus Christ." He continued: "Explorers had been to those regions, and big-game hunters, Arabs and traders, European officials and scientists, but no Christian had ever gone to tell of Jesus."

"The shame sank into one's soul," said C. T. Studd. "Why have no Christians gone?"

"Why don't you go?" God queried.

"The doctors won't permit it," C. T. hastened to defend himself.

The answer came: "Am I not the Good Physician?" – and C. T. Studd, his soul on fire for God, sailed for Africa, on the fifteenth day of December, 1910[3].

On the sixteenth day of July, 1931, C. T. died. One year later, at a memorial service at Ibambi, nearly ten thousand Africans gathered and an extraordinary fervour of rejoicing and re-dedication was wonderful proof that the work had been firmly built on the Lord and not merely on C. T. Studd's remarkable personality. The triumph of seeing Wabari and Wabudu jostling happily with Bazande and Medje, Mangbetu and Mayogo sharing testimonies with Marambo and Malika, was a mighty demonstration of the power of the Gospel to break down tribal barriers in a way that no political or philanthropic effort had achieved. "It was," as one observer remarked, "just a glimpse of the greater Day round the Throne, when every tribe and nation shall bow the knee before the Lamb!"

So the first decade of this African church was built on *sacrifice*: basically, the one all-sufficient sacrifice of the Son of God for the sins of the whole world, and secondarily the consequent sacrifice of the life of an intrepid missionary warrior, who gave up all that the world holds dear in order to take the Gospel of the Lord Jesus Christ to the uttermost parts. C. T. Studd accepted long years of separation from his beloved wife and daughters, accepted long years of physical suffering far from the medical aid that could have given him relief, and accepted long years of ceaseless toil – preaching, teaching, writing, translating – asking for no reward save that of knowing that he did his Master's will. Truly, he was a "living sacrifice – acceptable to God" and used for the salvation of thousands.

During the next decade, the young Mission that the

veteran had founded, with its defiant motto of abandonment to Christ, "If Jesus Christ be God and died for me, then no sacrifice can be too great for me to make for Him", and its clear cut goal, "to evangelise the remaining unevangelised parts of the earth in the shortest possible time", had to learn the absolute priority of *faith* for all its forward movement.

Two immediate and crucial needs faced the Mission in that year of 1931, when the founder died, and as the depression settled over the world's economy. These critical needs were men and money. Norman Grubb and his wife Pauline, C. T. Studd's third daughter, claimed from God *ten* new workers, by the anniversary of Studd's death, the sixteenth of July, 1932, and all the money needed to launch them. So sure were they that God had commanded them to make this claim, that they thanked Him there and then, and publicly declared their faith as fact.

The ten new workers came, sent by God; and tested, and provided for, they sailed for Africa by the Autumn of 1932[4].

From that moment, spurred on by faith, the WEC church, foreigners and nationals alike, set themselves the target of establishing local churches on indigenous lines, and of marching forward to complete the occupation of the "regions beyond", up to the boundaries of all neighbouring missions. This involved a six-fold expansion of the work, from ten thousand to sixty thousand square miles of territory. By faith, that target was achieved. Churches were established in each far-flung corner, from Malingwia to Lubutu, from Niangara to Opienge.

But then came the crunch. In the following decade, under the leadership of Jack Harrison, the young church in Congo, black and white, had to come to terms with God's command: "Be holy because I am holy."

Sacrifice, yes. Had not Jack himself had to sacrifice his ardent desire "to go and evangelise"? Full of eagerness to preach Christ, had he not instead to accept his leader's frustrating demand "to stay around and sharpen tools"? He had felt hedged in with thorns and nearly resigned from the Mission – but he did not. He discovered that the frustration he felt was not because of his leader's command, nor because of his circumstances. No: the trouble was in himself. From that moment, he allowed God to break him and make him "an instrument ... made holy, useful to the Master and prepared to do any good work" (2 Tim. 2:21).

Faith, yes. Had not Jack himself proved God over and over again, in providing for all personal and family needs through many years in Congo and on furloughs, and as he sought to "lengthen the cords and strengthen the stakes" so that the Gospel should reach every unevangelised tribe in the area for which the Government had made WEC responsible?

But now, Holiness. What was to be his reaction?

With the tremendous growth in numbers of those who had come to know and love the Saviour, there was urgent need for a parallel growth in depth of those who were to lead and teach these new converts. Personal Holiness through the work of the indwelling Holy Spirit became the one dominant message of all conferences. A special session was held for evangelists and leading Christians. Missionaries pleaded with them, from burdened hearts, urging them to bring out of their homes anything sinful or of a questionable nature, everything that was keeping them from putting Christ first in their lives, and that was spoiling their testimony to His power and victory.

The response was astonishing!

From the beginning, as the work of purging in the hearts of the evangelists took place, so came an immediate change in their message and teaching. They began to stress the necessity for the work of the Spirit in sanctification to take place in the life of every believer who had entered into Christ's work of justification. The Word began to cut the hearts of their hearers. Many faced the claims of the Holy Spirit but were unwilling for the cost. A great and almost devastating secession took place. Hundreds ceased to attend the meetings and began openly to backslide, returning to the attractions of the world around them. Even a number of evangelists fell away. The hearts of missionaries and spiritual Africans felt crushed by the blow, but from that very crushing came the wine of God's refreshing.

The Central Bible School was founded, at this time, to give in-depth training, to help deepen spiritual understanding and, in consequence, the holy and consistent living of Church leaders and members. Each one must be equipped to teach others also. The only prerequisite for entry to the school was a heart on fire with the Holy Ghost and a burden for the salvation of souls around. The early students could barely read and write, and their lack of ability to understand arithmetic was pathetic. So, in the first place, tremendous efforts were made to teach the three "R"s, in order to enable them to read and study the Scriptures. Then they were taught God's wonderful plan of redemption as revealed throughout the Bible, learned how to apply these truths in their daily lives, and were shown how to impart them to others. Simple though such teaching was, the standards were considered by some to be "so high" that numbers dwindled to five.

After much heart searching, a group of missionaries and a handful of spiritually-minded church leaders accepted responsibility to plead with God and believe for revival. At first, they met for a night of prayer once each month. As the burden grew, they added a monthly day of prayer. Conscious that they were not giving God all, they started to hold a day of prayer and fasting once each week. Still conscious of the urgent need of the Church for cleansing and filling, for, as someone put it, "power to walk in white", to bear a consistent testimony before the world, they began to meet for half-an-hour of prayer every lunch hour. Then, every evening at the end of the day's work, they also set aside an hour for prayer ... At that point, the Spirit came.

"To think that we have been privileged to live through these days of revival blessing!" one of the Bible School leaders wrote. "It is beyond anything we had imagined. We have longed, prayed, cried, agonised for revival, and God has done the 'exceeding abundantly'. We are only in its beginnings, for judgment begins where God says it does – at the house of God. He has been setting His house in order, purifying, cleansing, empowering by the Blood and the Spirit: now He will turn to the heathen, and who shall abide the day of His coming?

"Our people have had a revelation of the sinfulness of sin and the Holiness of God, and they know now, not in their heads but in their hearts, that 'without Holiness no man shall see the Lord'. Before it was, as it were, the missionaries' interpretation of the Word: now it is the Holy Ghost convincing them of the truth.

"Scores and scores have been absolutely broken before the Cross. The Holy Ghost has dug deep and brought to light the filth which had been buried away for years. There was no escape. They had to call a spade a spade: big and so-called 'little' sins had to be classified together. In the light of the Cross and a holy God everything looked vile – bad thoughts, criticisms against one's neighbour, pride in every form, lust in the thought life, worldliness in dress, etc.

"As the testimonies have been given, what joy, what peace, what radiance, what ecstasy, as the Holy Ghost came in and took possession. As testimony after testimony poured forth, so more and more there was a releasing of the power of the Holy Ghost. I for one have been caught right up into the glory of the whole thing and thought I would burst with sheer joy.

"The closer one approaches to God, the deeper the realisation of His Holiness and His standards.

"Who am I to be writing about Holiness?" the writer continued. "I need to get there myself. I am such a long way from being what I ought to be. However, like Paul, I press on toward the goal"[5].

*   *   *

Those of us who were there will never forget that day in July 1953, when the fire of revival fell at Ibambi. It was the time of the Friday evening fellowship meeting. Jack Scholes had just stood up to read the Scriptures, when suddenly we were all conscious of the rushing noise of an approaching hurricane. Senior Bible School students moved quietly round the hall taking down the shutters to avoid the danger of their being blown in. Idly glancing out into the dark night, I was aware that the palm trees stood erect, silhouetted against a moon-lit sky ... and there was no sign of the approaching storm, no scudding clouds, no trees bent to the ground by the violence of the gale-force wind.

Then came a tremendous shock as some great force struck the hall and all of us were shaken. There was a moment of intense silence. Then, some broke out in strong crying; some were thrown to the ground; some trembled uncontrollably; all were under the influence of a mighty unseen Presence.

"Words fail to describe it, but we know something now of what it must have been like on the day of Pentecost," wrote Jack Scholes afterwards, seeking to explain how the Holy Ghost had come down on the church in mighty power. The very building had been shaken as by a hurricane, though the still, silent palm trees etched against the clear, moon-lit sky not only proved the absence of a physical storm, but by nature's motionless gaze, even accentuated that inner storm.

All over the building, the Spirit took control. Men and women were shaken by a force outside themselves, a mighty force that they could not refuse nor gainsay. Some cried out for mercy. Some were physically thrown to the ground. Some appeared rigid, gripped as in a vice. Some shuddered uncontrollably, the very bench they sat on being rocked by the force.

People were under deep conviction of sin, crying out to God for mercy and forgiveness. Tears flowed. Sweat poured. Agonies were endured, as strong men sought to resist, as women sought to flee. Some fell to their knees confessing hidden sins, with no one but God listening to them. Others were thrown down on the cement floor, stretched out before God, bringing to the light things buried in their hearts of which they had hoped never to be reminded.

Events that previously had been considered as "weaknesses", such as bad temper or grumbling, irritability or complaining, were seen as *sin* as the Holy Spirit shone into hearts the pure light of God's Holiness. No corners were left in shadow. No black could be considered grey. Petty faults – cheating at an exam, skipping washing-up duty, going off duty ten minutes before the bell rang – became hideous in their sight, as they were contrasted with God's standard of purity. "Silly jesting" was seen to be as evil as "immorality, or ... any kind of impurity, or ... greed" (Eph. 5:3).

One woman cried out for mercy as the Holy Spirit revealed to her the sin of lying. She had been to the local store to buy a storm lantern, and had haggled over the price. When the shopkeeper had said that the cost was what amounted to eighty pence, she had declared that she did not have so much money, until he reduced the price to sixty-five pence. She had then paid with a note worth a pound! We may smile at what seems just an exaggeration in a particular situation, easily understanding that her declaration of inability to pay only meant her unwillingness to pay so much, wanting the change doubtless for something else. But this was no time to smile. The Holy Spirit called that deception *sin*, however small or insignificant we may think it; and sin cannot be tolerated by a Holy God in a member of His family.

Even as this woman confessed that sin and sought forgiveness in the substitutionary death of the Saviour, so the Holy Spirit led her on to see a far greater sin that she had been quite unaware of ten minutes earlier. She cried out in anguish of heart and for some time she could not speak, so filled was she with shame for what had been revealed to her.

That same shopkeeper, who had sold the storm lantern, was a white-skinned Greek trader; his assistants were local black-skinned Congolese tribesmen. Thursday by Thursday,

Naganimi and I had walked together the mile and a half to those local stores, on our weekly free afternoon from Bible School studies. Always Naganimi had spoken to the African assistants, hopefully expecting me to witness to the European trader; but she herself had never spoken to "the white man" of his soul's need of the Saviour, and the Spirit showed her this as *sin* – not only the sin of colour-consciousness, but also the sin of not caring sufficiently for an individual's salvation.

I was shattered as I overheard her broken-hearted confession to the Lord, her pleading for forgiveness, her willingness to go at once and speak to that trader of Jesus and His great love. If *that* was sin, where did I stand? How many times have I ever spoken to shop assistants of their need of forgiveness for their sins?

Another woman, also a Bible School student, wept bitterly as the Holy Spirit reminded her of her spirit of grumbling. The men students brought firewood from the forest early every morning to the school's kitchen. There, the women built the fire and put on the porridge for breakfast, before going in for the first period of studies, consecutive teaching through the New Testament given by the principal. Often the men were late, arriving with the wood just as the bell went for school. They were just able to slip into the classroom during the singing of the opening hymn; but the women still had to get the fire going and so were often late for the teaching. They grumbled. If *that* was sin, where did I stand? How often did I grumble with far less justification?

An evangelist and his wife broke down under the Spirit's revelation of what their argumentative tempers caused the Saviour to suffer. They had a tiny baby, who was fretful and very difficult to feed. The little one kept them awake at night, and the husband became irritable with the loss of sleep. His wife answered him back angrily that it was his child as much as hers, and he did nothing to help her in caring for it. Their tempers were often frayed, and they criticised each other outside the home to any sympathetic ear that would give heed to them. The Holy Spirit revealed to them their lack of love and of trust, their selfish desire for their own peace and sleep, and consequent failure to bother with each other's needs. If *that* was sin, where did I stand? How often was I irritable when patients came to call me at meal times, or a nurse broke one of the precious thermometers?

A Mayogo woman had had difficulties in school because she was the only woman from her tribe. No one was willing to plait her hair for her. I had tried to help, with a somewhat comical outcome, and all had laughed, searing the hurt deeper into her spirit. The Holy Spirit revealed to her that this hurt was sin, because it stemmed from self, her desire to be wanted and welcomed; and at the same moment, He revealed to two others, a Bazande and a Mubari woman, that their action too was sin, as their unwillingness to help this Mayogo woman in the plaiting of her hair stemmed from self, their pride in their tribal ancestry. All these sought each other's forgiveness at the same instant! and I asked myself: "What about me? How proud am I of being white, of being a doctor, a missionary – maybe unconsciously proud but, nevertheless, proud – and surely that also stems from self?"

A carpenter, down on the ground, crying with strong tears, inarticulate under the hand of God, suddenly got up and left the hall, going purposefully out into the night. Shortly afterwards, he returned with a hammer, a packet of nails of mixed sizes, a plane, and some lengths of timber under his arm. He laid the lot down by the table in the front of the hall, and cried out: "O God, forgive me!" He had stolen these from the station workshop, and had had no peace until he returned them.

During the days that followed, much lost property was returned to its rightful owners – tools, materials, books, clothing, foodstuffs, even live chickens. A tailor brought back a bag of scraps of material that he had taken home from work as being "too small to be of any use". Some men asked time off work, as they had to go seventy-five miles through the forest to Wamba, to return stolen goods to Government workshops or to Greek traders. The authorities were dumbfounded and did not know how to react or what to do.

"Never before," they said, "have we ever seen anything like it!"

* * *

Reading of "the fifty-nine" revival, the great Ulster awakening of 1859, one is amazed at the similarity of the pattern the Holy Spirit followed in dealing with men in Northern Ireland as a hundred years later He dealt with men in the heart of Africa. In a history of those days in Ireland, the writer speaks of the deep conviction of sin, the severe conflict with Satan, the unique delight in the Word of God that led to super-abounding praise, impassioned prayer, unspeakable joy and intense love; and he goes on to tell of lives becoming conformed to a Scriptural Holiness.

"Conviction [of sin] became so awful," he continued, "that, unable to lock it up in the breast, the sinner was compelled to cry out in agony, confessing the iniquity of his sin, and, feeling himself sinking into perdition under the burden of guilt, fell down from weakness of body produced by the intensity of his guilty distress. Cries of 'Unclean! Unclean!' frequently rent the air as this conviction manifested itself in many"[6].

During the Welsh Revival of 1904, Eifion Evans reports: "Friday night's meeting was characterised by the intensity of conviction felt in it. Scores found themselves on their knees, unable to utter a syllable, and quite overcome with a sense of guilt. Some of these fell in a heap and others cried out pitifully and loudly in their desire for mercy. Meanwhile Evan Roberts was in spiritual agony, the perspiration pouring from his brow, as he prayed that God would glorify His Son and save sinners. So the meeting continued as a mighty spiritual upheaval until the dawn of a new day. People lost all sense of time, and forgot their need for food, and were seemingly kept from physical exhaustion at their daily work"[7].

The Holy Spirit worked in the same way in the Belfast shipyards through the ministry of W. P. Nicholson in 1922–25, when not only were hundreds of men saved by the grace of God, but also, as a result of the Holy Spirit's work in their hearts convicting them of sin and leading them to repentance, a whole warehouse had to be set aside to receive the stolen goods that men returned. Mr Thorn, an elderly man in charge of tools and equipment at Harland and Wolfe shipyards, remembers how he had to go to the management to ask for premises to hold all that was restored by the converted men[8].

A report from another mission in Lisburn in County Antrim at the same time comments: "Business people have had debts, long since written off as irrecoverable, paid in full. Money wrongfully used has been returned. At the last petty sessions court, there was only one case down for trial ... a unique experience. There has been a great diversity in the types of character reached. Drunkards and gamblers have had the chains of their sins snapped. Formalists have been quickened into new life. A holy concern has gripped and changed the careless"[9].

In the Isle of Lewis, through the ministry of Duncan Campbell, God worked similarly in 1950. One report tells us: "A solemn hush came over the church one night ... The service closed in a tense silence ... The awful presence of God brought a wave of conviction of sin that caused even mature Christians to feel their sinfulness, bringing groans of distress and prayers of repentance from the unconverted. Strong men were bowed under the weight of sin and cries for mercy were mingled with shouts of joy from others who had passed into life"[10].

In 1971, press headlines in a Canadian newspaper read "Saskatoon: vortex of revival" and gave the following report: "What began as a typical evangelistic campaign mushroomed into a spiritual awakening. The Holy Spirit moved quietly and powerfully: church leaders and Christian workers confessed sin and were reconciled to each other; business men in the city were surprised when people called to pay for stolen goods; broken homes were restored, alcoholics and drug addicts delivered, and countless numbers freed from the bondage of self and satanic oppression to witness effectively for Christ."

So in Ulster, Wales, Scotland, Canada, as in Congo/ Zaire, "the blessed Holy Spirit was doing what He came to do, to convict of sin and to reveal the Saviour," wrote Norman Grubb. Through each of these reports runs the strand of conviction of sin. Men and women were made to see sin in its reality.

It is indeed true, as John Owen says: "A man must abhor himself before he can serve God aright." In the words of Dr J. I. Packer: "If our concern is with practical Christian living today [that is to say, how to live a holy life], a Puritan model of godliness will most quickly expose the reason why our current spirituality is shallow, namely the shallowness of our views of sin"[11].

Always, in revivals, the Holy Spirit creates in the hearts of Christians a hatred of sin, not just of its consequences. The ten commandments take on a new role in their lives, revealing God's standards for Christlike conduct. Coupled with Christ's own words in the sermon given on the mount (Matt. 5–7), the Christians begin to allow the Holy Spirit to compare their individual lives with the pattern given in Scripture, and conviction of sin grows. People see anger and irritation as sin. Wrong desires and covetous jealousy are seen to be sin. Discontent, grumbling, unbelief, wanting one's own way, all manifestations of self and pride, are recognised as they truly are – *sin*.

The Potter is at work, removing the gravel that mars the vessel.

During seasons of revival, Christians come under deep conviction by the Holy Spirit and the awful revelation of the pain that our sins cause our Saviour. The quick retort of self-vindication, the subtle use of words to say one thing yet mean another, the nursed hurt despite the outward shaking of hands, the easy excuse that "everybody else does it, so what?" the plausible reasoning to make wrong look right – all these are seen to be *sin*.

The Potter is still at work, now removing the finest grit that mars His planned vessel.

It is God Himself who reveals sin to be sin. It is the Holy Spirit in my heart that causes me to be "uncomfortable" about that which He wishes to show me is wrong. I have found that I do not have to search my heart to seek out wrong things. They become clearly wrong to me as I open my heart to the influence of the Spirit:

> Search me, O God, and know my heart;
>   test me and know my anxious thoughts.
> See if there is any offensive way in me,
>   and lead me in the way everlasting (Ps. 139:23,24).

Once anyone begins to sense that some action or thought or desire in their lives is wrong (that is, wrong for them), it is useless to argue about it, or discuss it with others, or seek to excuse it by circumstances, custom or culture. It just has to go, or one has no peace.

One also finds that one does not necessarily come under condemnation by hearing someone else's confession of sin. It could be that what one confesses does not yet bring another under conviction for the same act. The Spirit moves in each heart, revealing and convicting as each one is ready to receive and respond. He becomes to us like a wonderful "private tutor", a school master who cares for each of His pupils individually, and is willing to give infinite time to the training and perfecting of each life given into His care.

*   *   *

When I was seeking to help some of my senior students in the medical college in Zaire, the teaching ministry of the Holy Spirit became very clear to me. I tried to illustrate this truth to the young men by an easily understandable African parable.

"For three years, a child had been attending a local primary school under the tuition of a very poor, irresponsible school master. In Grade one, the child had learned that two plus two equals five, and all further teaching was based on this premise. Furthermore, the lazy teacher made no effort to mark homework but, rather, ticked every line as correct, and added a routine ten out of ten at the end. Content that he was progressing satisfactorily, though in truth learning nothing, the child made no effort and whiled away his days in his own way.

"Due to some unrecorded circumstance, the day came when the parents entered their child for another school where, unknown to them, there was an excellent standard of teaching and individual tuition.

"'I'm ready for Grade four,' announced the unabashed youngster to his new teacher.

"'Really?' queried the teacher, with a slightly sceptical rise of his eyebrows. 'We'll see,' he added gently, as he allowed the boy to take his seat with the other fourth formers.

"Conscientiously marking his class's homework that evening, the teacher had to give the newcomer zero, out of the possible ten marks, for his mathematics, based as they were on the initial wrong assumption that two plus two equals five. Next day, the same result.

"Angrily, the boy grumbled that his new teacher was hopeless, that he had his knife into him, that he might as well quit and go back to the primary school where he always received full marks, 'Ten out of ten.'"

We may smile at that incident, but in our Christian lives how many of us make the same mistake of blaming our teacher rather than ourselves when we fail to reach the required standard? After years in the devil's school, where anything goes, and where no one knows right from wrong, the first days in the new school are often very difficult.

Leaving the old school and entering the new may well be exciting. One's name is entered in the register; one receives the right to wear the school uniform; one is allocated a place in the dormitory, in the dining hall and in the classroom; one is welcomed by name and made to feel at home; but one does not receive the coveted leaving-diploma then! No, that has to be worked for over years of concerted study.

Likewise, when one is first converted and one's name is written in the Lamb's Book of Life, one is proud to wear the uniform ("clothe yourselves with the Lord Jesus Christ" Romans 13:14), and the badge ("you are marked in Him with a seal" Ephesians 1:13), but one has not yet received the diploma ("Holy to the Lord" Exodus 39:30). The potential, the promise, the purpose are all clear, but the practical outworking in the daily life has yet to be experienced.

From the start, the un-learning of the wrong already imparted by the previous teacher is as difficult as the understanding and absorbing of the new material being taught. The first week in the Christian life may seem one great shattering failure, our conscience many times each day convicting us of transgressing the new rules and of missing the mark in the new studies. The devil whispers in our ears that we are not converted at all! He laughs at us that we could even think we were. He taunts us with our failures, saying that these prove we are still in *his* school.

Never! Nothing could be further from the truth. It is a lie. When we were in the devil's school, he did not care how we behaved or what we did. Everything "went" with him. Whatever we did or thought or said, he gave us an unremitting ten out of ten. Now my disappointment at receiving only one out of ten, or three out of ten, is translated in my mind, by the devil's cunning, as meaning that I had not become a pupil in the new school. On the contrary! It is this very mark that my conscience gives me, that proves I *am* in the new school and under the tuition of the Holy Spirit. No one else would bother to mark my daily conduct and point out to me where I had failed to reach the prescribed standard of Holiness. Only He, the Holy Spirit, cares enough for my progress, and is willing to concern Himself on my behalf to watch and comment on my progress. It is He who has re-activated my conscience to be able to respond again, after the deadening influence of the previous searing experience.

So now, when I realise that I have failed, and when my conscience accuses me of wrongdoing, if I go at once to my Tutor, the Holy Spirit, to ask Him in what I have offended and to seek His help to put it right, I find Him always ready and willing to explain. Not only will He convince me of my error, and show me what is right, but He will also give me grace to thank Him for so doing, and to make the necessary corrections.

Slowly, if I am willing to be diligent in learning, I shall progress until I begin to approach the eight out of ten mark, maybe for a few consecutive days of rejoicing! Then, imperceptibly, my Tutor (the Holy Spirit) moves me up a class, as it were, and starts to teach me something new. If I am not giving diligent care, I may so easily be caught off-guard, and land myself in trouble, back with two out of ten. The devil is just waiting to pounce, and with glee he assures me that all my efforts are of no avail: it is useless for me to think I'll ever be a consistent, victorious Christian.

"Write yourself off," he says. "Come back to me and enjoy being yourself, and stop thinking you can ever become anything else. You, holy? What a joke!"

And I am sorely tempted to believe him, in the heartache of repeated failure.

But I must not listen to him. He is a liar from the beginning, and the father of all lies (John 8:44). He is deceitful and the accuser of the brethren (Rev. 12:10). He never cared enough even to look at my homework, never mind to mark it carefully, nor to be available to show me what was wrong and to instruct me as to how to put it right. No, indeed! In such a situation, the fact of the low mark is a proof that one's conscience is now alive, and able to hear and respond to the Spirit's prompting and checks.

* * *

So it is only the Holy Spirit who can make us want to be holy, revealing what things are sin (conviction) and giving us a hatred for these things and a great desire to be rid of them (true repentance). As I grew up, I had only hated the consequence of sin; as I sought to go on with God, however, I had a growing hatred of sin itself.

Then an urge began to grow in me to put right all I could of the wrong that I had inflicted on others – restoring what was stolen, confessing to what was untrue, forgiving where I had borne a grudge, loving where before I had felt hatred. This "putting right" of wrongs committed can never merit or earn forgiveness, any more than we can gain salvation by good works: but it is the outcome of a contrite heart. As the Holy Spirit convinces us of sin, and grants to us godly repentance, so also He brings to birth in us this desire to make restitution.

There are times when there is nothing we can do to repair the damage we have caused, yet it is still true that a "broken and contrite heart, O God, You will not despise" (Ps. 51:17). His forgiveness is dependent only on the finished work at Calvary. Spirit-given repentance only brings about my personal identification with the redeeming grace of God – nothing else. As the Spirit of God works in me that "broken and contrite heart", I shall seek to express it by "fruit in keeping with repentance" (Matt. 3:8; Luke 3:8), deliberate turning from sin, resolute seeking by God's grace to be done with the hateful thing that caused me to fail, and where possible, by reparation for the past.

Whether there is a *crisis* start to this life of "being made holy as He is holy", or not; whether there is a date when one first agrees with God's verdict on one's life and of one's need of the ministry of the Holy Spirit in sanctifying grace, or not, there *must* be a *continuance*, a daily dying to self, an hourly "being filled" with the Spirit. When Paul declared, "I have been crucified with Christ and I no longer live, but Christ lives in me," the Greek words, I believe, could equally well be translated: "I am being crucified with Christ ... so that Christ may continually be living in me" (Gal. 2:20).

Pastor Ndugu, a godly African church elder, first made this truth real to me, some four years after I started my missionary service in Congo. Things had gone wrong at Nebobongo. I was very conscious that my life was not what it should have been. I was losing my temper with nurses, being impatient with the sick, getting irritated with workmen. Everything had got on top of me. I was overwhelmingly tired, with an impossible work load and endless respons-ibilities. Suddenly I knew that I had to get away from it all and sort myself out and seek God's forgiveness and restoration, if I was to continue in the work.

The pastor had seen my spiritual need and made all the arrangements for me to go to stay in his village for a long weekend. I felt crushed by my own wretchedness and oft-repeated failures. I knew I was quite unworthy of the title "missionary", and I yearned to know the secret of a closer walk with God and of a new in-filling by the Holy Spirit. On the Sunday evening, I went to the pastor and his wife, as they sat together in the palaver hut by the embers of the fire, and asked him to help me. I did not have to explain what I meant; he knew.

Opening his Bible at Galatians 2:20, he drew a straight line in the dirt floor with his heel. "I," he said, "the capital I in our lives, Self, is the great enemy."

Stillness reigned.

"Helen," he said quietly, after a long pause, "the trouble with you is that we can see so much Helen that we cannot see Jesus."

Again he paused, and my eyes filled with tears.

"I notice that you drink much coffee," he continued presently, apparently going off at a tangent. "When they bring a mug of hot coffee to you, wherever you are, whatever you're doing, you stand there holding it, until it is cool enough to drink. May I suggest that every time, as you stand and wait, you should just lift your heart to God and pray ..." and as he spoke, he moved his heel in the dirt across the I he had previously drawn, "... Please, God, cross out the I."

It was very still.

There in the dirt was his lesson of simplified theology – the Cross – the crossed-out I life.

Crucifixion – death to self – the Cross in the life of a Christian, or as Paul worded it, "I have been crucified with Christ and I no longer live, but Christ lives in me" (Gal. 2:20).

For over twenty years now, I have sought, however imperfectly and falteringly, to follow that godly pastor's simple "rule of life", allowing the Master Potter to have His way, undoing and remaking the vessel.

Just as the presence of grit mars the perfection of a jar, so the presence of sin in our lives spoils the beauty of the "earthen vessel" that God is creating to contain "the treasure" of the in-dwelling Christ (2 Cor. 4:7).

If a man cleanses himself from the latter [that is, from all the grittiness of sin], he will be an instrument for noble purposes, made holy, useful to the Master and prepared to do any good work (2 Tim. 2:21).

This sin, for which the Saviour sweated great drops of blood, for which He suffered the agony of being forsaken by His Father, for which He was crucified, mars the vessel that the Heavenly Potter is moulding for special service, and so it must be dealt with, drastically and irrevocably. Our God spares no pains to root out of us all the dross, all the impurity, all that would cause defect or decay, the whole rottenness of our old nature, for He wills to make us "a radiant church, without stain or wrinkle" (Eph. 5:27). God said of Paul: "This man is My chosen instrument to carry My Name ..." (Acts 9:15). So is each one who has been adopted into God's family, and He wants each vessel to be perfect.

3

Second step – Love

Why should we love God?

You want me to tell you why and how God is to be loved?

I answer that the reason for loving God is God Himself. As to how He is to be loved, there is only one measure: It is immeasurable!

God deserves to be loved because He gave Himself for us, unworthy of it as we are. Yet being God, what greater gift than to give Himself? Hence this is surely the greatest claim that God has upon us, "because He first loved us" (1 John 4:19). He thus deserves the response of our love in return.

Who is so worthy to be loved? Surely it is He of whom the Spirit confesses (1 John 4:2), saying, "You are my Lord, for You do not need anything from me" (Ps. 16:2). This then is the true love of the Majestic God, who does not seek His own advantage (1 Cor. 13:5).

And to whom did God direct such a pure love? "When we were still sinners, we were reconciled to God" (Rom. 5:10). Thus did God love us, freely so.

To what measure did God love us? John tells us: "God so loved the world that He gave His only begotten Son" (John 3:16). Paul adds: "He did not spare His own Son, but delivered Him up for us all" (Rom. 8:32). The Son declared of Himself: "No one has greater love than he who lays down his life for his friend" (John 15:13).

This then, is the claim which the Holy One has upon the guilty, and the Supreme Being has upon all miserable mankind.

Bernard of Clairvaux[1]

3 Second step – Love

"You don't touch her but over my dead body!"

* * *

It was 1964. Rebel insurgents had taken over the north-eastern province of the Congo (previously known as the Belgian Congo, and later as Zaire), driving out the national army and imposing a fierce military regime over the terrified villagers. The occupying forces had a proud bravado born of drugs, drink and witchcraft. They felt themselves to be invincible, and cruelly crushed any tiny spark of suspected resistance. Savage beat-ups, barbarous mutilations and ultimately indescribable murders were the order of the day.

One terrified student from our male nurses' school at Nebobongo came back to us from a weekend with his parents in the nearby township of Isiro, distraught and unable to talk for several days. Then he told us that "the streets were running with blood" and of how he and other youths had been rounded up to dig enormous pits by day for the burial of the dead by night – huge communal graves for upwards of five hundred unrecognisable corpses.

Rumour told us that a local chieftain had been captured, tortured, and then systematically flayed alive, and . . . I could hear no more. My stomach became a tight knot. Revulsion and fear fought battles with my mind by day and in my dreams by night.

A pregnant woman was seized from our maternity complex, bound and thrown up on to a truck. As the soldiers drove off, we could not shut out her terrified screaming as they kicked her and stabbed at her with their spears.

Life became a living nightmare, but we had to go on living.

Whenever we could, we met together in the church or in my home or under the trees, to pray and read the Word of God and sing His praises, and so we kept sane, and God graciously replaced fear with peace.

After ten dreadful weeks, the tide of war turned. The country's President, Kasa-Vubu, called in mercenary soldiers to serve under the national army's chief-of-staff, Colonel Mobutu. Morale rose. Discipline improved. The army started to re-take the country, repulsing the guerillas, many of whom died in the new offensive.

"How can we die?" they asked themselves. Had they not been promised that, through the power of their initiation rites, no bullet could harm them? In fact, "Bullets will be turned to water," they were assured, "by the power of Lumumba!" who became their patron saint.

The only way the witch-doctors could explain their loss of power was by the supposition of a stronger witchcraft in the hands of the advancing national army. But who was the witch-doctor who would dare to challenge the power of Lumumba and his Simba troops?

This reversal had occurred with the arrival of white troops. It did not take much ingenuity to arrive at the conclusion that the white "doctors" had worked the needed "dawa" to break the power of the guerilla forces. So the rebels turned against every white doctor in their territory with frightening ferocity.

One never-to-be-forgotten night, 29 October, 1964, seven or eight armed bullies, cursing and merciless, stormed my home. They pulled the place to bits, stealing all they could lay their hands on, before they turned on me personally. Somehow, up to that very minute, I had managed to believe that they would never strike a white woman. I was unprepared for their vicious attack, and utterly terrified. I tried to flee, rushing out through the front door and throwing my storm lantern to Hugh, the seventeen-year-old student nurse who was on duty with me that fateful night. My diary continues:

> I ran round the side of the house, halfway down the pathway to the toilet. I thought they'd go, as they had completed the inspection for which I understood they had come. I could hear their coarse laughter . . .
>
> They followed me, flashing powerful torches, shouting that I had escaped and was hiding something from them. I flung myself under some bushes in the thick mud and pulled my dressing-gown over my white face and feet, praying they would go, my heart nearly bursting with fear and near-panic.
>
> But in ten minutes they found me, dragged me to my feet, and struck me across the face, searching around me for what I was hiding – they just did not appear to understand that I was only hiding myself from them! I reeled and my glasses went. My heart was pounding with fear: my mouth parched and dry. Another forced me again to my feet. The leader cursed me terribly, and struck me again over the head with a rubber truncheon. I was shoved back to the veranda. A second younger nurse had fled, but Hugh, held by two armed men, stood in the courtyard, watching me with transfixed horror.
>
> As I stood trembling against a pillar of the veranda, almost mentally paralysed, the lieutenant stuck his pistol in my face and demanded that I should declare . . . that he hadn't touched me or some such thing . . . and that Lumumba was the only Saviour for the people. Others persuaded him not to shoot me (I almost wished he would and finish it – my heart was with Jesus and a quiet peace was mingling with the frantic fear . . .)
>
> At that moment, Hugh, wrenching himself free from the two soldiers who held him, hurled himself between me and the lieutenant, shouting defiantly, almost triumphantly, "You don't touch her, but over my dead body!"

"Musimugusa, isipokuwa kwanza utakaniuwa!"

They turned on Hugh, with horrendous savagery – and I was sick.

They kicked his apparently lifeless body about like a football – and I almost fainted.

That Hugh should give his life to save mine was a demonstration of love almost too great for me to comprehend. He had not long been a Christian, and I had had the privilege of being one of the group that had visited his village two years before to tell them of the great love of the Creator God, who had sent His Son to this world to die for us. The teenager's heart had been deeply touched that Almighty God could know him, and love him so much that He had been willing to die to redeem him; and he had made a very definite, clear-cut response to give his life to serve his new-found Saviour.

Hugh was not dead, as I had thought, but I was not to know that for a long time to come. He was terribly bruised and wounded, but he recovered. That particular night, about an hour after I had been driven away captive, he had regained consciousness sufficiently to crawl painfully the hundred yards to the hospital. Here he woke the night staff to report, "They have taken our doctor!" before relapsing into merciful unconsciousness.

By God's grace, he eventually made a full recovery, but the fact remains that he had willingly "given his life" in order to save mine.

"My command is this: Love each other as I have loved you. Greater love has no one than this, that he lay down his life for his friends" (John 15:12,13).

* * *

That he *loves* God – isn't this, surely, the immediate positive sign in the heart of a new believer, that the Holy Spirit has indeed brought him into the state of regeneration? As the Spirit convinces us of sin and leads us to repentance, so also

He pours out into our hearts (Rom. 5:5) the LOVE of God. This is the work of Christ on our behalf because He loved us:

This is how we know what love is: Jesus Christ laid down His life for us (1 John 3:16).
The Son of God, who loved me and gave Himself for me (Gal. 2:20).
This is how God showed His love among us: He sent His one and only Son into the world that we might live through Him (1 John 4:9).

and we find ourselves loving Him:

We love [Him] because He first loved us (1 John 4:19).

We have naturally no such love toward God in our hearts. On the contrary, before entering into our new relationship as God's children by adoption, we tend to hate all that is good and holy and of God, because our natural man is rebuked and made to feel uncomfortable in the presence of Holiness. When, however, we become members of God's family, the Holy Spirit pours into our hearts the very love of God, and we find ourselves loving Him with His love.

This love is holy, and pure, and altogether good. It may be almost without emotional content, because it is beyond the concepts of human emotion. It is not sentimental, nor superficial; it absorbs our whole being. This new power of love finds expression, firstly in a previously unknown desire to worship God Himself, and then, secondly, in outreach to all around us. Jesus Himself told us that this would be *the* way that others would know the reality of our new experience of salvation: "A new command I give you: Love one another. As I have loved you, so you must love one another. By this all men will know that you are My disciples, if you love one another" (John 13:34,35).

Christ gives us that new commandment at the end of a

very dramatic chapter, in which He shows us clearly two levels in which we can express this new divine love to one another. He was actually teaching His disciples some very deep and discerning lessons in leadership, lessons that are entirely different from the usual worldly ones on the same subject. In the world, a leader is a Somebody, somebody before whom the world around bows down and to whom they show utmost respect.

God's way for Christian leaders (and all of us) is so different. In the world's estimation, it is a way "down" rather than "up". At the supper table in the upper room, when Jesus partook of the feast of the Passover with His disciples, He, the very Son of God, "took off His outer clothing, and wrapped a towel round His waist" in order to pour water into a basin, and knelt and washed the disciples' dusty feet. He did the most menial task, that not one of His disciples had been willing to undertake, a task usually performed by the lowest of the slaves, someone on the bottom rung of the so-called social ladder. Our Lord did it willingly, naturally, and with no loss to His dignity or His authority – because He loved them. "You call Me 'Teacher' and 'Lord', and rightly so, for that is what I am. Now that I, your Lord and Teacher, have washed your feet, you also should wash one another's feet" (John 13:13,14). Christ showed that true spiritual leadership is revealed in servanthood.

In the same chapter, linked directly with this object lesson is another lesson, with a similar command at its close. Sitting at table with our Lord was one who even then was plotting to betray Him, Judas Iscariot. Christ performed a very simple act, so simple that we are likely to miss its shattering significance. As was the custom at such a feast, the host took a choice morsel from the communal dish, dipped it in the bowl of sauce, and offered it, as a sign of special recognition, to "the favoured one". On this occasion, Jesus offered the sop to Judas. Knowing that Judas was filled with contempt and angry disappointment and possibly even hatred, and that he was about to betray Jesus to the Pharisees, who would crucify Him, yet, to the very end, our Lord loved him and demonstrated that love by this simple act.

Then Christ said to His disciples, "My children . . . A new command I give you: Love one another. As I have loved you, so you must love one another" (John 13:33,34).

The disciples were bewildered by the very simplicity of the two acts, as Christ washed their feet and as He offered Judas the dipped morsel. Christ never merely theorised: He put into practice what He wanted us to learn. Firstly, He took the place of the lowest slave doing the most menial task of foot-washing to reveal the true nature of real service. Then, at the very moment when Judas was planning the betrayal, our Lord took the dipped morsel and offered it to him, to reveal the true nature of real love. These two acts are but the two sides of the same coin. As Christ in-dwells us, so will His love work in us and through us.

When we first enter into this new relationship with God, becoming His adopted children, love is wonderfully real to us, and we are very conscious that "we love Him who first loved us". It is a joy to sing:

Loved with everlasting love, led by grace that love to know:
Spirit breathing from above, Thou hast taught me it is so!
Oh, this full and perfect peace! Oh, this transport all divine!
In a love which cannot cease, I am His and He is mine.

and:

My Jesus, I love Thee, I know Thou art mine;
For Thee all the pleasures of sin I resign.
My gracious Redeemer, my Saviour art Thou;
If ever I loved Thee, my Jesus, 'tis now!

Yet, as we go on in the Christian life, there may come a time when we are not quite so sure of how to express that love. As it deepens, it appears to draw us above and beyond the normal concepts of love, even, as it were, out into a great abyss of love, where all is dark and no words can express it. We may even fear that we have lost our love. Some may even question if they have ever truly loved at all. Is this what Paul was hinting at when he wrote of "the love of Christ ... that surpasses knowledge" (Eph. 3:19), and what the hymn writer sought to express?

> It passeth knowledge, that dear love of Thine,
> My Jesus, Saviour, yet this soul of mine
> Would of Thy love, in all its breadth and length
> Its height and depth, its everlasting strength,
>   Know more and more.

The more we seek to understand "the incomparable riches" of the Grace of God, who planned our redemption from before the foundation of the world, because of His "great love for us", the more conscious we become of the shallowness of our love for Him. That we ought to love Him, as we consider all He has done for us through His death on the Cross as propitiation for our sins, we are never in doubt; but whether we do love Him, in actual daily fact and experience, we may well begin to question. A deep yearning in our innermost being "to know Him more clearly, love Him more dearly and follow Him more nearly" is probably all to which we dare lay claim. Those who have such feelings, are, as A. W. Tozer so aptly puts it, "athirst to taste for themselves the piercing sweetness of the love of Christ"[2].

As the Psalmist puts it in Psalm 42:1,2:

> As the deer pants for streams of water,
>   so my soul pants for You, O God.
> My soul thirsts for God, for the living God.

Tozer goes on to say, "To have found God and still to pursue Him is the soul's paradox of love, scorned indeed by the too-easily-satisfied religionist, but justified in happy experience by the children of the burning heart. St Bernard stated this holy paradox in a musical quatrain that will be instantly understood by every worshipping soul:

'We taste Thee, O Thou living Bread,
And long to feast upon Thee still:
We drink of Thee, the fountain head
And thirst our souls from Thee to fill.'"

Two hundred years later, Richard Rolle, while a student at Oxford, was greatly influenced by St Bernard, and is reputed to have said to one of his friends, "Let us love burningly!" Yet, in his writings, such as in the "Song of Love", there is a great sighing to know how so to love:

My song is a sighing, my life is spent in longing for the sight of my King, so fair in His brightness. So fair in Thy beauty! Lead me to Thy light and feed me on Thy love! Make me to grow swiftly in love and be Thou Thyself my prize[3].

So we should not be surprised if we also have difficulties in "knowing how to love God", however much we know that it is our bounden duty to love Him.

Each of the great mystical lovers of our Lord – Francis of Assisi, Julian of Norwich, Catherine of Genoa, Teresa of Avila, Jakob Boehme, Benjamin Whichcote, Miguel de Molinos, Madame Guyon, to name just a few, throughout the centuries – sought the fulness of deep peace and joy in loving God, who so wholly loved them. And found, as they grew closer to God, a deeper yearning and a more passionate desire to *love* Him truly in a manner more worthy of His great love for them. Perhaps Jonathan Edwards sums up all their most intense aspirations when he says:

The more a true saint loves God with a gracious love,

the more he desires to love Him, and the more uneasy is he at his want of love to Him: the more he hates sin, the more he desires to hate it, and laments that he has so much remaining love for it ... The kindling and raising of gracious affections is like kindling a flame; the higher it is raised, the more ardent it is; and the more it burns, the more vehemently does it tend and seek to burn. So that the spiritual appetite after Holiness, and an increase of holy affections, is much more lively and keen in those that are eminent in Holiness, than others; and more when grace and holy affections are in their most lively exercise than at other times[4].

When an African housewife kindles a fire to cook the evening meal, she angles three large logs end to end, and into the gap left between them stuffs light twigs and brushwood. These can be ignited without much difficulty, and crackle and sparkle with joyful noise and bright flames. All can see and hear that the fire is going, yet at this stage it cannot boil a kettle! There is very little heat generated by this initial burning. However, as this dies down, the large outer logs are pushed yet closer together to support the cooking pot. The fire, having entered into the heart of the logs, now burns deeply and steadily, silently and invisibly, giving forth the needed heat.

When we first come to the Saviour, the flood of joy that fills us may well break forth in singing and lighthearted service, which can be easily seen and heard by all around. As the work of the Holy Spirit burns deeper into the life, however, though there will perhaps be less exuberance, there will be more and permanent evidence of the reality of our love for our Saviour.

God only offers us two ways of expressing our love for Him. In the first place, by obedience to His every known command:

Whoever has My commands and obeys them, he is the one who loves Me (John 14:21).

He who does not love Me will not obey My teaching (John 14:24).

And these commands include the "new command" of John 13:34 that we "love one another".

Secondly, we show our love towards God by our service one for another:

I was hungry and you gave Me something to eat, I was thirsty and you gave Me something to drink, I was a stranger and you invited Me in, I needed clothes and you clothed Me, I was sick and you looked after Me, I was in prison and you came to visit Me.

And when they asked Christ what He meant, He concluded:

Whatever you did for one of the least of these brothers of Mine, you did for Me (Matt. 25:35–36; 40).

And this surely demonstrates the meaning of Christ's words after He had washed His disciples' feet in that Upper Room at the feast of the Passover:

"Do you understand what I have done for you?" He asked them. "You call Me 'Teacher' and 'Lord', and rightly so, for that is what I am. Now that I, your Lord and Teacher, have washed your feet, you also should wash one another's feet. I have set you an example, that you should do as I have done for you" (John 13:12–15).

* * *

There were so many others, like Hugh, during my years in Congo/Zaire, who really put all this into practice – maybe with less dramatic heroism, but nevertheless as penetratingly real in their devotion. Tamoma, Pastor Ndugu's wife, was one of them. Frail already at fifty years of age from chronic bronchiectasis, she was utterly uncomplaining and totally selfless in her "home-making" for Ndugu and their three children. When the church met us, the day I first arrived at Ibambi, she was there, slightly bowed, with her hands typically held together in front of her, her lovely smile with the deep dimple on the left cheek, her "alive" eyes shining out her welcome.

It was nearly six in the evening, just as dusk was falling, when the Mission truck eventually forged its way into the village, after two long, exacting days struggling through the forest from the Ugandan frontier, along appalling mud roads. All the forty-four Bible School students, with their many little children, came across the palm-lined road from their compound, up the avenue of variegated-leaf bushes, to gather under the WELCOME banner outside Jack Scholes' home. Seven foreigners, white missionaries, had just arrived! Four were back from furlough, two had come as short-term visitors, and I was the new arrival. They sang to us; speeches were made; there was more singing and hand-shaking; and yet more singing ... We were almost too weary to keep on our feet – and I was almost too happy to be able to hold back the tears.

Pastor Ndugu stepped forward, a tall, upright man with only the slightest brush of grey touching his receding hair, and he seemed to look straight at me with a smile filled with a radiant warmth, as he first greeted us as a group, and then welcomed me personally.

"We, the church at Ibambi," he said, "welcome you, our child, into our midst."

Six weeks of enormous effort on the long journey from England to Central Africa had enabled me to learn just enough Swahili to get the gist of that one sentence, and as I did so, I almost forgot my carefully-rehearsed sentence of reply: "Ninafurahi na furaha kubwa kuwa hapa katikati yenu!" – "I have great joy to be here among you" – and my tears overflowed in the infinite sense of joy that filled my heart.

They surged around us, shaking our hands a hundred times, chatting and laughing . . . and slowly I slipped to the back of the veranda, leaning against the wall, emotionally overwhelmed, yet still watching and listening.

Suddenly, quietly, there was dear Tamoma, with an arm round my shoulders, her gentle eyes looking deeply into mine, soft laughter twitching at the corners of her sensitive mouth.

"Ninakupenda," she said – "I love you" – and hugged me! She didn't know me. She'd never met me before. She couldn't communicate with me. But she loved me!

She had prayed for years that God would send a doctor to help them in their great physical needs. When she had heard that a student doctor was interested, she had redoubled her prayers for God's good hand to be upon that student that He might give her success in her exams and certainty regarding her call. When the news had arrived that the exams were at last safely over, and the young lady doctor was in the Mission's headquarters being prepared for future service, Tamoma prayed on that there would be no proverbial "slip between the call and the ship". Days seemed to multiply, and months to become years, with no sign of the promised doctor: but Tamoma never gave up her prayers that God's will would be fulfilled in His own perfect timing.

And I had at last arrived. And she loved me!

From that moment, Tamoma and Ndugu took me into their hearts and their home, as their own child. For me, it was my first introduction to a Christian family who obeyed literally Christ's command to His disciples: "Love one another", that thereby "all men will know that you are My disciples" (John 13:35).

That a senior woman of different culture and a different language from mine was willing to offer me Christ's love without first "getting to know" me, to evaluate whether I was worth loving or not, was a quite extraordinary experience. Nothing else in my first month honestly caused me culture shock, but this one act – a warmhearted hug, a straight look, a gentle comment: "I love you" – *this* caused me a lot of personal heart-searching. Would I have loved Tamoma with the same unquestioning warmth if our situations had been reversed? Was it merely a matter of the proverbial British reserve coloured by Western culture – or was it really something much more fundamental, a lack of holy Christ-likeness on my part?

"But God demonstrates His own love for us in this: While we were still sinners, Christ died for us" (Rom. 5:8).

Christ loved me enough to die for me while I was yet His enemy. If God had waited for me to learn to love Him before He died, I would never have been saved. I knew that with my head, but when I met someone who behaved in such a completely Christlike way, I was amazed. In the twenty years of my life in Congo/Zaire, Tamoma's love for me only grew deeper and stronger. Her home was always open to me, her friendship was unchanging. When I found myself spiritually discouraged or physically overtired, the obvious place to turn for love and comfort, be it also for rebuke and teaching, was Adzangwe, the village of Pastor Ndugu and his wife; and they were always available to God to channel to me that which I needed.

In July of 1960, three weeks after the declaration of Independence and twelve hours after the great evacuation of "white foreigners" from the north-eastern province, I was again sharply reminded of the reality of the love of God in the Christians around me. I was the only European left at our village of Nebobongo, and a lorry-load of National Army troops had driven through at dusk, chanting ribald songs and threatening, with coarse laughter, to return during the night "to enjoy the white lady's company".

My over-active imagination would not be stilled as I got ready for the night. Fear had come into my home. I lay and tossed on my bed, allowing Fear to grow larger and take possession of my reasoning faculties. A rat ran across the rafters and I shot upright, certain there was someone in the house. An owl threw a shadow across the moon-lit room, and I froze with the thought that I was being watched through the window.

I could stand the tension no longer. In desperation, I crawled out of bed, got down on my knees, and simply asked God to hold me close to Himself. As my heart-beat began to steady down, and quietness regained possession of my vivid imagination, I asked God that, if it were possible, He would produce someone – I had no suggestion as to whom or how or from where – to stay in my home with me until the political crisis was past.

Bang!

I nearly died! My mouth parched, I thought my heart would stop.

"This is it!" my taut mind reasoned. "They've come!"

Again, a quiet knock at the back door, that sounded like a pistol shot in the strained silence of that night.

Somehow I stumbled down the corridor, but it was all I could do to make my voice come out of my frozen lips.

"Who's there?" I struggled to call out.

"It's only us!" whispered back two obviously female voices.

Sagging at the knees, I opened the door in shattered relief, and welcomed Taadi, our evangelist's wife, and Damaris, our head midwife.

"Come in, come in," I urged them, shutting the door quickly and firmly behind them and leading them through to the sitting room. I sat down with my head in my hands, trying to recover composure from the wave of shock that had assailed me, and then, dizzily, I asked them why they had come.

"Well," said Taadi, "I woke from sleep, and the Lord said to me very clearly 'Go to the doctor, she needs you,' so I got up and came."

"That's exactly what happened to me!" exclaimed Damaris. "And, actually, I felt guilty because last evening I had thought about coming to stay with you, but I was afraid that you would think it was cheek, so I did nothing."

I looked at the two of them, awed at the way God had answered my prayers so immediately through these two dear, loving women. I told them of all that had gone through my mind in the last three hours, and of how I was actually on my knees, at the very moment when they knocked, praying to God for someone to stay with me.

We all three felt humbled and amazed at being part of the wonderful out-working of God's will. We laughed and cried and hugged each other, and then thanked God for His goodness to us. I made up beds and we had hot chocolate together before settling down to sleep out the rest of the night.

There were others. During the months of the Simba uprising in 1964, so many stood by me. The savagery of the suffering on all sides made each one of us face up to God's claim on our lives in a new way. Were we ready to die? Could we literally, meaningfully, say with Paul, "To me to live is Christ, and to die is gain"? Was there anything in the way, so to speak, any unresolved conflict in our minds, any unforgiven sin in our practice, any lack of assurance in our spirits? The urgency of the situation made us realists, and we daily sought to have "clean hands and a pure heart". Even if the participants were unconscious of it, this practical search after living Holiness showed itself in simple acts of love.

The first Sunday after the rebel army had invaded us, Basuana preached his heart out on Romans 8:28–39, emphasising that "all things" – including rebel captivity and unknown atrocities – "do work together for good to those who love God" and that indeed "none of these things" can move us or distress us because nothing, absolutely nothing, can separate us from the love of Christ. And I knew, as I listened to him from the back of the church, that he had poured his whole heart into that sermon because of his love for *me* – to comfort and strengthen me as he sensed the fears in my heart.

A few weeks later, amidst seventeen wild and armed youths, John and Joel climbed into the back of the truck, in which I was being forced to drive these rebels to Wamba. It had been an appalling night, heavy dark clouds blotting out the moon, sweeping rain driven by a blustering gale, the road surface churned into a sea of mud. The vehicle had no lights, no self-starter, no windscreen wipers. Nervously fiddling with the pin of a hand grenade, the diminutive, teenage "lieutenant" of the gang had ordered me to drive into the courtyard of a local palm oil factory, to search for petrol and oil and, if possible, to get the lights repaired. Ordered out of the truck, I stood a few yards from it, alone in the dark.

That was when I first realised that John and Joel were with me. I sensed them, rather than saw them, one on either side of me.

"Go away from me," I hissed to them. "They will kill me. Don't stand with me!"

They made no move.

I repeated my message urgently, thinking that they had not understood.

"Doctor," came their quiet reply, "that is why we are here. You shall not die alone!"

Half-an-hour later, when the rebels had driven off in our repaired truck, leaving the three of us standing there alone in the rain, alive despite every indication that we were going to be brutally murdered, Joel spoke for all three of us, as he said, "I felt like one of Daniel's three friends in the burning fiery furnace. Surely a fourth stood with us whose form was like that of the Son of God!" They had gone through that experience with me purely out of Christlike love. They did not need to be there!

Agoya, our evangelist, used to "appear" from nowhere, whenever rebel soldiers accosted me: eight o'clock one evening when I was teaching in night school; ten o'clock one morning when I was operating in theatre; another day at lunchtime; another when I was playing games with the children. He was just there, solid and unflinching, giving me enormous moral support – simply because of the love of God "poured into his heart by the Holy Spirit". A comment in my diary reads:

> Tues. Oct. 27. Three rough, crude fellows arrived at the
> school demanding "Bwana". "That's me," I said! "No, we
> want the white man," and before I could answer, one of
> them raised his club to strike me. Even before I could
> think fast enough to dodge the blow, Agoya was there,
> between us.

That was it. Always there when needed, guided by love,
willing to suffer rather than see me attacked.

During the ten week British postal strike early in 1971,
another church elder stood by me, in very different
circumstances, yet with the same sensitivity born of godly
love. I had been seconded by my own Mission to work in an
inter-mission medical project in a neighbouring district, on
the foothills of the mighty Ruwenzori mountain range.

One evening, as I was sitting at home preparing lecture
material for the next day, a knock at the front door heralded
the arrival of two church elders. I invited them in and served
coffee and biscuits, while we chatted about one or two local
events. Then the senior man leant forward, head bowed
slightly, looking at the floor.

"Doctor," he started, rather hesitantly, "please do not
think we have come to intrude, but we have noticed that you
have received no mail for several weeks. Is something
wrong? I mean, is there anything we can do, any way we can
help you?"

I laughed, albeit a little nervously, surprised at their keen
observation, and I explained as best I could about my
nation's postal strike. I knew all the lurid details from the
weekly American journals of my medical colleagues at
Nyankunde!

They listened courteously, but I became aware that my
words were not informing them of anything new. I began to
suspect that they had already talked to others and heard it all
before. Anyway, why was I bothering them with my

country's problems? They had enough of their own! When I stammered to a halt, Pastor Butso coughed slightly and, looking up at me with his charming smile, held out a bulging envelope.

"Would you please accept this," he asked graciously, "from our church family? We realise that you can have had no financial allowance from your home since no letters come ..." and then he went straight on, before I had time to gather my wits, "... and when eventually your money comes, *please*, we do NOT want you to return this. It is not a loan but a gift" and he added in a rush: "because we love you!" What could I say?

Out of their poverty they had given – and given generously. Their giving had the fragrance of the woman, whose act Jesus called "beautiful", when she broke the alabaster jar of very precious ointment and anointed His head (Mark 14:3–9). Their giving savoured of the sacrifice of the poor widow, who, Jesus said, had given more than all the wealthy donors to the temple treasury, because she had given all she had (Mark 12:41–44).

I had tears in my eyes as I sought to thank them, but they brushed aside my comments, suddenly embarrassed, and started talking about the forthcoming Easter services and our college choir's part in the worship of that day.

* * *

As I think of the generosity of those Africans, how, out of their extreme poverty, they showed me the love of God by their unstinted goodness to me, I am reminded of that lovely hymn of Frances Ridley Havergal:

Thy life was given for me; Thy blood, O Lord, was shed,
That I might ransomed be, and quickened from the dead:
Thy life was given for me: what have I *given* for Thee?

In the last line, the author asks herself the first of a series of very searching questions. "What have I given for the Lord Jesus Christ, compared to all He has given to me?" with the inference that this would show how much she truly loved Him.

How can we measure what we "give" to God to show Him our love? I think of an African parent who brought a chicken to me two weeks after I had done a life-saving operation on his little child. Some might say that the value of a chicken hardly equalled the value of all the training that had been necessary to enable me to undertake that delicate operation, and that therefore the gift was inadequate as a thank-offering.

If that were so, then there is no way that I can show God the thankfulness of my heart for His great gift to me of redemption: anything I offered would be inadequate! But I believe, in God's eyes, the two acts, my operating and their chicken, *were* of comparable value. We had each given ALL we had. In evaluating the two gifts, the attitude of heart was the important factor.

The sadness of today's prevalent attitude in so many situations – "what do I get out of it?" – is in stark contrast to the attitude of love stirred by the Holy Spirit in a believer's heart – "what can I give to help in this situation?"

"God so loved the world that He gave . . ." no end, no time limit, no measure, no calculation. His giving could only be called a reckless abandonment of love. Do I love Him in like measure, and am I willing to show it by a similar reckless abandonment? Even though others may call the giving up of my rights to my own selfish ambitions sacrifice, do I believe that it is in fact only privilege?

Am I willing . . . to give up time or sleep or watching a television programme or going to a football match, for example, to do some small service to another in need, just because I love my Saviour? Am I willing . . . to give up a high salary or prospects of promotion, and my own private ambitions, in order, for example, to go and serve others in some needy corner of the mission fields of the world, or to supply what is needed to enable someone else to go? Love, as an expression of Holiness, will stir such "giving" in my life. In the last line of the next verse, Frances Havergal's question is, "Have I *left* aught" – "to show You how much I love You?"

Have I left anything, just because of my love for my Saviour? We sometimes hear of a Moslem man losing his job, his home, his friends, even his life because he accepted the Lord Jesus Christ as his Saviour. He is willing to "leave" all because of the intense love for God that fills him, a pure, holy love poured into his heart by the Holy Spirit. And I am forced to ask myself: am I equally willing to "leave all"? or has God two standards – one for those in Moslem lands, and another for those in so-called Christian lands?

Is my love for God such that I gladly "leave" the habits of my old life, when these prove incompatible with the Holiness of my new Friend? I must decide who is going to run my life, Christ or myself, and this decision will be influenced by the reality of my love – is my love for God greater than my love for myself?

God gave us the ten commandments, to assist us to develop habits in our new Christian lives compatible with His Holiness. These rules have been likened to the "blinkers" on a horse running in a race, which prevent him from being distracted by movements on the sidelines and encourage him to keep looking straight ahead. Christ increased the dynamism of this godly "rule of life" by insisting that it applies to that which motivates us as well as to our overt actions. Not for one minute did He allow us to think that by the new Covenant in His blood were the Old Covenant rules abrogated. No, indeed! Those ten commandments provide clear, practical rules for daily living, and I must "leave behind" any habits from my old life that are inconsistent with His standard for holy living. I am no more free to choose the rules for such holy living, when I enter God's family, than a football player is free to make his own rules for play, when he is invited to become a member of his county team! Do I love my God enough to say "Yes!" to His rules, even when this means saying "No" to my own desires?

Frances Havergal's third question to herself: "What have I *borne* for Thee?" makes me realise how little I know of suffering for my Saviour. So much of what I think I "suffer" for love of my Saviour is actually the result of my own pride or selfishness or pigheadedness. When I am left out of a group or of a conversation, it is easy to think that it is because I am a Christian, rather than to realise it is because I am bossy, or self-centred, or have a superior attitude. When I feel "hurt" by others' reactions to me, this should be a warning that the old I is not crossed out! Christ in me may be grieved by a situation, but He is not merely "hurt". Having "hurt" feelings can so often be just a selfish reaction. If what I "suffer" is honestly caused by Christ's in-dwelling, then I should be proud of God's friendship and that He considers me "worthy to suffer shame" for His Name's sake.

In communist lands today, many Christians are willing to face and accept imprisonment, solitary confinement, cruelty, hard labour, exile – rather than deny Christ as their Saviour. This is an expression of the reality of their love for their Saviour. How would I fare under such a regime?

Peter told Jesus that he would face even death with Him, but we all know how later he denied his Saviour with oaths and curses, declaring that he did not know Christ – just because he was scared stiff that if he owned the Master as his friend it might cost him his life.

What would you and I have done? To refuse to laugh at smutty jokes; to stand up for truth and honesty at work; to remain unemployed rather than take the only available job if this involves regular work on a Sunday; these may be some of the "costs" for today's Christian. Is my love for God so real, that I would have no difficulty in owning Him as my Lord in any such circumstance ... or would I be tempted, as Peter, to deny Him?

If God asked me to suffer sickness or pain for a period of time, could I say with conviction, "We know that in all things

God works for the good of those who love Him, who have been called according to His purpose" – or would I grumble and wonder why God let it happen to me? Could I thank God for trusting me with the experience, even of severe illness, and seek His grace to learn more of Him through it, so that I in turn could help and encourage another – or would I demand healing, thinking of such as my "right" because I am a Christian?

This attitude of heart and mind, that can joyfully trust God in all circumstances, can only take possession of me as I allow the Holy Spirit to fill me with love for my Lord. The promise is to "those who love Him". Let us remind ourselves that we only love Him because He first loved us and because He has poured His own love into our hearts in order that we have wherewith to love Him. When this amazing love of God takes over and controls my life, I can truly accept "all things" from His hands without murmuring or dispute.

When Frances Havergal further asks, "What have I *brought* to Thee?" I feel so small and inadequate. Whatever have I that I could possibly bring to God to show Him my love?

Do you remember the words of Christ to the sleeping Peter in the Garden of Gethsemane? "Could you not keep watch for one hour?" In the hour of His greatest need, Christ craved the close companionship and loving support of His dearest friends – just when He needed them most, they slept!

God longs, above all, for us to bring Him our love. It is by obedience to His first great commandment: "Love the Lord your God with all your heart and with all your soul and with all your strength" (Deut. 6:5) and also to His new commandment: "Love one another. As I have loved you, so you must love one another" (John 13:34) that we witness to others that we are Christians. "All men will know that you are My disciples if you love one another," is His word to us. This "love" is to be self-giving involvement for the good of others rather than ourselves, caring for them and serving them. "As I have loved you," said our Lord, was to be the model of our loving.

> Do nothing out of selfish ambition or vain conceit, but in humility consider others better than yourselves [wrote Paul to the Philippians]. Each of you should look not only to your own interests, but also to the interests of others.
> Your attitude should be the same as that of Christ Jesus: Who, being in very nature God, did not consider equality with God something to be grasped, but made Himself nothing, taking the very nature of a servant, being made in human likeness. And being found in appearance as a man, He humbled Himself and became obedient to death – even death on a cross! (Phil. 2:3–8).

Christ longs that the loving service that we give to others should be brought as an offering to Him, in gratitude for all that He has given for us. Some will know the hymn of G. Kendrick which expresses this so well:

1. From heaven You came
   Helpless Babe,
   Entered our world,
   Your glory veiled;
   Not to be served
   But to serve,
   And give Your life
   That we might live.

2. There in the garden
   Of tears,
   My heavy load
   He chose to bear;
   His heart with sorrow
   Was torn,
   "Yet not My will
   But Yours" He said.

3. Come see His hands
   And His feet,
   The scars that speak
   Of sacrifice,
   Hands that flung stars
   Into space
   To cruel nails
   Surrendered.

4. So let us learn
   How to serve,
   And in our lives
   Enthrone Him;
   Each other's needs
   To prefer,
   For it is Christ
   We're serving.

and the chorus to each verse, bringing in our response:

> This is our God
> The Servant King,
> He calls us now
> To follow Him.
> To bring our lives
> As a daily offering
> Of worship to
> The Servant King[5].

Frances Havergal finishes her hymn on the same note, this need of offering our life's service to God as an act of worship: "Thou gav'st Thyself for me; I *give* myself to Thee." She had caught a vision of God's great purpose for her life. She knew that we were created by God, not only to *live* a purposeful, meaningful life, abundant and rich, in fellowship with Himself, but also to *give* ourselves to Him and to each other. Our whole life would then become an expression of love, "to the praise of His glory", worshipping and serving Him in our glad surrender.

Are we not in danger of turning all this upside-down? Have we lost sight of God's purpose for our life that it might be one of self-*giving* love? Have we not become over-whelmingly selfish, seeking to "get" rather than to "give"? The contrast between God's plan and our practice is almost unbelievable. To right this wrong, God *gave* Himself for us at Calvary. The holy Lamb of God, without spot or blemish, died in our place, as our Substitute. God longs for the response of our hearts, that we should seek Him first and His righteousness, *giving* Him His rightful place in our lives, putting Him first in everything and crowning Him King, not just in hymnody, but in reality.

As the Holy Spirit continues to work in our hearts and lives, transforming us into conformity to the image of God's Son, not only will He burn up the sin and dross in our lives, but He will create in us an intense longing to *give* God all we are and have, because "we so love Him who first loved us".

Grace Reese Adkins sang:

By and by when I look on His face,
His beautiful face, His thorn-shadowed face,
By and by when I look on His face,
I'll wish I had given Him more
– more, so much more –
More of my life than I e'er gave before.

Yes, we shall indeed wish we had given Him more. As God's love pours into us, we long to *give* – to give more to Christ and more to others. This urgent desire to *give* to others replaces the previous desire to *get* for oneself.

During the 1859 revival in Northern Ireland and the 1904 revival in Wales, under the ministry of W. P. Nicholson in the 1920's and of Duncan Campbell in the 1950's, reports came from all sides, telling of people not only under conviction of sin, but also filled to overflowing with love. One such report told of "more than one hundred souls in this parish whose hearts God has graciously touched since the movement started. Their daily living is fragrant, their fellowship blessed, their love vital and glowing – as beautiful a progeny of grace as one has ever seen"[6].

God worked in exactly the same manner in the centre of Africa on the fringe of the great Ituri forest, in the hearts and lives of black men and women, as He did in the islands of the Hebrides among the crofters and village folk of Scotland, and in Ulster among the dockyard workers and city dwellers of Ireland, and in Wales among miners and chapel-goers.

This love that flowed into the lives of each one touched by the fires of revival showed itself in an intense desire to *give*, to give themselves to God and in service to one another. As an example of this, Damaris stands out in my memory above all others. In the mid-1920's, when she first heard the Gospel from the fiery preaching of C. T. Studd, she was a quiet, gentle, forest woman of limited education. Damaris and her husband joined C. T.'s "roving band" to be trained as evangelists. In 1933, they trekked south to take the Gospel to the Opienge area. Damaris' husband found the standard of Holiness demanded of God's missionary servants too high; and when she failed to give him children, he took a schoolgirl as a second wife. Disciplined by the church, he remained unrepentant, and became arrogant and aggressive. He rejected Damaris, who drifted away and sank back into the ways of her pagan village, until she became the mistress of a young Belgian district official.

Cooking his meal one day, she overheard a Christian giving his testimony to her white master. Suddenly the past rushed back into her mind and heart, and overwhelmed by the love of God "who gave His Son to redeem fallen mankind", and by the shattering ingratitude of her proud and sinful heart, she wept brokenly, confessing her sins and seeking God's gracious pardon.

Overnight she became conscious of what it means "to be a new creation". God's holy love just poured into her and filled her with peace and joy. She eventually made her way back to Ibambi, and subsequently to my home at Nebobongo.

"Would you try to train me to be a midwife?" she asked humbly. "I just want to do something to serve others, and to show them how much God loves them."

And that is what she has been doing ever since, for nearly thirty years now. Not only is she a good and conscientious midwife, but also she is a radiant Christian, through whom pours the love and patience of Christ, day and night, seven days a week, fifty-two weeks a year. She is always available to those whom she seeks to serve.

Nothing is ever too much trouble. She never thinks in terms of time off, and has never demanded a rise in salary. She is endlessly patient and loving with the pupil midwives in her care, always believing the best when others have given up all hope for a change of heart in some recalcitrant student. She even became a Chief in the local girls' Campaigner Clan, that she might get alongside the girls the better to understand and help them, though she laughingly told me that her greying hairs hardly matched her uniform!

To all her other responsibilities, Damaris voluntarily added that of the care of orphaned babies until they were old enough to enter the children's home. These tiny mites grew up in the sunshine of her unstinted love, when every thing in life seemed to be against them. She nursed them through pneumonia; she loved them back to life from dysentery; she almost invented food for them in times of hunger. She washed them, fed them, clothed them. From their youngest days, she prayed for them and taught them about the Lord Jesus Christ. She sat up with them when they were sick; she sang them to sleep when they were crotchety. Nothing ever seemed too much trouble where "her babies" were concerned. They were, as it were, her own family, and she poured upon them all the love that God constantly poured into her. As they grew up, she yearned over them and never ceased to pray for them, almost breaking her heart over anyone that "went the wrong way". Her love was indeed an undying fire, fuelled by the in-dwelling Holy Spirit of God.

Does this make the standard of the thirteenth chapter of Paul's first letter to the Corinthians a little clearer to us, so that it no longer seems an unattainable dream?

Love is patient, love is kind.
It does not envy, it does not boast, it is not proud.
It is not rude, it is not self-seeking, it is not easily angered, it keeps no record of wrongs.
Love does not delight in evil but rejoices with the truth.
It always protects, always trusts, always hopes, always perseveres.
Love never fails.

God's Holiness is like a consuming fire. Not only will it burn up all the dross and impurities in our lives – the impatience, pride, anger – leading us to true godly repentance, but also it will melt the stony and soften the hard in our lives – the self-seeking, self-vindicating, self-righteousness – filling us with true godly love. I need to pray: "Spirit of the living God ... melt *me!*"

We can use hardness of heart as a defence mechanism, protecting us from becoming too involved in another's pain. It can enable us to remain outside situations without being hurt by them, even when we give an appearance of being involved, but such hardness and stony-heartedness can keep others at arm's length.

The unstinted love of my African friends is in such contrast to this. They are never unwilling to love to the uttermost, never afraid of being hurt by giving too much of themselves.

Their love is so patently real – a simple, radiant love, that understands without cynicism, that trusts without suspicion, that forgives without harbouring hurts, that strengthens without demanding reciprocal care. Their love knows no limits. It enabled them to stand beside me before the menacing spears of an advancing rabble; to suffer with me when I was so ill that I did not even know that they were there, until they had nursed me back to life; to die for me if by that means they could have spared me one ounce of what I suffered. Their love mirrors Christ's, as Paul portrays it in that marvellous thirteenth chapter of his letter to the Corinthians. They are so rarely proud or boastful, critical or envious even when they have ample cause to be; they are patient and kindly, courteous and loyal, even when those with whom they have to do are being most un-Christlike, demanding, impatient or self-assertive.

Is it not true that as we seek to put into practice "the crossed-out I life" of Paul's teaching to the Galatians: "I have been crucified with Christ and I no longer live, but Christ lives in me. The life I live in the body, I live by faith in the Son of God, who loved me and gave Himself for me" (Gal. 2:20), so God's Holiness will be expressed in the warmth and generosity of our love, both to Him and to others.

4

Third step – Obedience

You call Me "Teacher" and "Lord" and rightly so, for that is what I am (John 13:13).

Our Lord never insists on having authority; He never says – "Thou shalt." He leaves us perfectly free – so free that we can spit in His face, as men did; so free that we can put Him to death, as men did; and He will never say a word. But when His life has been created in me by His redemption, I instantly recognise His right to absolute authority over me. It is a moral domination – "Thou art worthy . . ." It is only the unworthy in me that refuses to bow down to the worthy.

If our Lord insisted on obedience He would become a taskmaster, and He would cease to have any authority. He never insists on obedience, but when we do see Him we obey Him instantly. He is easily Lord, and we live in adoration of Him from morning till night. The revelation of my growth in grace is the way in which I look upon obedience. We have to rescue the word "obedience" from the mire. Obedience is only possible between equals. It is the relationship between father and son, not between master and servant. "I and My Father are one." "Though He were a Son, yet learned He obedience by the things which He suffered." The Son's obedience was as Redeemer, *because He was Son*, not in order to be Son.

Oswald Chambers[1].

4 Third step – Obedience

"Do you ENJOY ... keeping the speed limits?"

* * *

Recently I was at a medical conference, and during the tea interval was in conversation with a colleague.

"What are you doing these days?" he enquired.

"Well," I answered a little hesitantly, "I'm trying to write a book."

"Oh," he exclaimed, "what about?"

"Well," I began, slightly embarrassed as I realised that several others had turned to listen to us, "on what it means to be holy in today's world."

"And what exactly is your thesis?" he probed.

"I think I want to write about such practical things as keeping the speed limits," I replied, thinking just how hard I was finding it to put my thoughts into words in a succinct and clear manner, as I had just started *this* chapter.

"Do you?" he demanded.

"Basically, yes, I do," I acknowledged.

"But do you *enjoy* ... keeping the speed limits?" was his parting shot, a little cynically I suspected, as he turned away to join another group.

As I drove home later, I thought over what he had said. Did I enjoy obeying the law, or did I only do it out of fear lest I should see a headline in the local newspaper: "Missionary doctor charged with speeding"? Did I drive with one eye on the speedometer and the other on the rear-view mirror looking out for a police car – or did I enjoy obeying the law

Living Holiness

and so drive in a relaxed way, certain that I would be within the limits?

Certainly obedience to the law for the sake of duty is good but can be pretty cold and legalistic and lacking in joy. If my obedience sprang from a true desire to please God, presumably I would enjoy the exercise.

The Holy Spirit, in His gracious work of sanctification in our hearts, gives us certain specific gifts that we may be holy and pleasing to God in our daily lives. Firstly, He gives us the gift of conviction of sin, and with it the ability to repent. Secondly, He pours into our hearts the love of God, thus enabling us to love God and our fellow men. Thirdly, He gives us the desire to obey God's Word and commandments, and the ability to do so, *with enjoyment*, in the little as in the bigger things of daily life.

Fourthly, as we shall see in the next chapter, the Holy Spirit gives us the privilege of realising that we are God's servants, chosen to be His ambassadors in this world in which we live, and He then gives us the ability to undertake that service in a manner wholly pleasing to God.

There is a temptation in the Church today to short-circuit the work of the Holy Spirit, and try to go from step two to step four, without bothering about step three. I am well aware that we cannot actually divide up our lives like that, into neat compartments, and that these four "steps" are continuous, and overlap each other with no fixed borders. Perhaps these "steps" are rather like the hoofs of a galloping horse, where all four are essential, repeatedly essential, until the race is finished, and it is often practically impossible to see the order in which they move!

The steps in our Christian life do not necessarily come consecutively, nor is one completed before the next begins. Certainly they will all be needful until our spiritual race is done; but they help us to see and understand that there is an orderly progression of thought and action in the process of sanctification.

Christ Himself clearly states that "If anyone loves Me, he

will obey My teaching" (John 14:23), and He also states the converse as being true: "Whoever has My commands and obeys them, he is the one who loves Me" (John 14:21), so that we can know that *the* way of showing the reality of our love for our Saviour is in obedience to His words.

Some would argue that to serve God *is* to obey His commands. Did He not command us: "Go into all the world and preach the good news to all creation" (Mark 16:15)? Therefore in throwing ourselves wholeheartedly into such service do we not show Him our love by our service, which is in turn but obedience to His commands?

That is possibly true, but if that service is a means to an end, if it is "in order to" show Him my love, or "as a means to" thank Him for His grace and salvation, it can so easily degenerate into a programme of contract-bargaining.

That just cannot be. There lies the danger of not recognising each step in the Spirit's ministry in our hearts to make us Christlike. He wants to make us holy; and indeed that is God's will for our lives. God's Word says, "It is God's will that you should be sanctified" (1 Thess. 4:3), and that must mean to be Christlike, as only Christ is actually holy and without sin.

Christ Himself never ceased to tell His disciples throughout His three years of public ministry that He was always activated by the desire to *obey* His Father and to fulfil His Father's will. Even when that obedience meant going to His death at Calvary, we can overhear Him say in prayer to His Father, in the Garden of Gethsemane, "Yet not as I will, but as You will" (Matt. 26:39).

Paul underlines this, when he stresses that we are to have the same mind as our Saviour: "He humbled Himself and became obedient to death – even death on a cross" (Phil. 2:8).

In other words, all we do in God's service should stem from our earnest desire to *obey* Him, rather than only from a desire to show Him that we love Him. The two may often appear to be the same, but we do well to make firm the foundation on which we build our endeavours towards Holiness.

Can I illustrate this point from two Old Testament stories of one event, in the first of which David, the king, wishes to serve God to show Him his love and things go sadly wrong, and in the second, the same thing is done out of obedience to God's Word, and all goes well?

Saul has died, and David has become the king. With the armies of Israel, David then conquers Jerusalem and turns it into his capital. Furthermore they defeat the Philistine armies, who some years previously had captured the Ark of the Lord from the Israelites. The Ark is central to the worship of God's people, and all had felt a great sense of loss when it was taken from them. David now determines to bring the Ark to Jerusalem.

He prepares with great care to give maximum honour to God. A new cart pulled by new oxen is made ready to bear the Ark, led by the priests, and David, with an enormous guard of honour, accompanies it on its journey. Suddenly, an ox stumbles and one of the priests puts out his hand to steady the Ark, to prevent its falling.

God struck the man dead.

"The Lord's anger burned against Uzzah because of his irreverent act; therefore God struck him down and he died..." (2 Sam. 6:7).

David was horrified. Why had God done this? Had he not only wanted to please God and to honour Him? How could he ever bring the Ark up to Jerusalem?

We are not told who went to David and explained to him God's law concerning the Ark and how it was to be moved from one place to another, but someone must have done so, probably reminding David of how the Ark had first been made "according to the pattern given to Moses in the mountain".

Bezalel made the Ark of acacia wood ... He cast four gold rings for it and fastened them ... Then he made poles of acacia wood ... and he inserted the poles into the rings ... to carry it (Exod. 37:1–4).

Then we hear the rules given for carrying the Ark when the camp moved:

> When the camp is to move, Aaron and his sons are to go in and take down the shielding curtain and cover the Ark of the Testimony with it ... and put the poles in place.
> The Kohathites are to come to do the carrying. But they must not touch the holy things or they will die (Numb. 4:5,6,15).

Furthermore, when the princes give gifts of oxen and carts to help the Levites to carry the Tabernacle during the long marches in the wilderness, Moses gives these to the Gershonites to carry the curtains and coverings; and to the Merarites to carry the planks and poles; but he does not give any to the Kohathites "because they were to carry on their shoulders the holy things, for which they were responsible" (Numb. 7:4–9).

So David tries again!

This time, he asks the Levites to be responsible for organising the march, with the Kohathites carrying the Ark on their shoulders "according to the Word of the Lord". The Levites also contribute musicians and choristers, and every so many paces, they sacrifice to the Lord, for David says, "It was because you, the Levites, did not bring it up the first time that the Lord our God broke out in anger against us. We did not enquire of Him about how to do it *in the prescribed way*" (my italics). And the record continues: "And the Levites carried the Ark of God with the poles on their shoulders, as Moses had commanded in accordance with the Word of the Lord" (1 Chr. 15:13, 15). There was tremendous rejoicing, as the Levites sang and played, and the Ark was brought safely to Jerusalem to the place that David had prepared for it.

You may think that is a lot of fuss about nothing, yet it

embodies such an important principle that God tells the story twice in great detail, both in the prophetic record in 2 Samuel 6, and again in the priestly record in 1 Chronicles 13 and 15. Obviously David was willing to humble himself and learn the lesson that Saul had failed to learn:

> Does the Lord delight in burnt offerings and sacrifices as much as in *obeying* the voice of the Lord?
> To *obey* is better than sacrifice, and to heed is better than the fat of rams.
> For rebellion is like the sin of divination, and arrogance like the evil of idolatry.
> Because you have rejected the Word of the Lord, He has rejected you as king (1 Sam. 15:22,23) (my italics).

Are we willing to learn this lesson? God wants, above all else, *our obedience to His will, if we would show Him that we love Him.*

And this obedience, if it springs from the right motive of love, will be joyous and not grievous. Christ Himself rejoiced to do His Father's will, even when that will led Him to Calvary. We read in the prophecy of Psalm 40:

> I desire to do your will, O my God;
> Your law is within my heart (Ps. 40:8; Heb. 10:7).

Even as He was going to Calvary, to suffer the appalling agony of being made sin for us and therefore separated from the Presence of His Father whose "eyes are too pure to look on evil", it is said of our Lord that "for the *joy* set before Him" He "endured the Cross, scorning its shame" (Heb. 12:2) (my italics).

He was indeed fulfilling the commandment to *obey*. God's first commandment to us is that we should love the Lord our God with all our heart and soul and strength; but we have disobeyed this, as God's other laws. Jesus stressed that He came into the world to fulfil His Father's will. He was sent and commissioned by God to be obedient, and by His perfect obedience to nullify our great disobedience. We disobeyed; but Christ fulfilled all the law and the commandments by His perfect obedience in supreme love for His Father; and thereby paid the debt owing to God for our gross disobedience.

What triumph there is in the absolute submission of the Son in obedience to the Father! And this obedience of Christ is to be our pattern if we would be like Him, and be holy as He is holy. We are to give Him this obedience not as unwilling slaves but as His friends: "You are My friends," said our Lord, "if you do what I command. I no longer call you servants, because a servant does not know his master's business. Instead, I have called you friends, for everything that I learned from My Father I have made known to you" (John 15:14,15).

Such willing, joyous obedience, given in love, demands my being available to God twenty-four hours a day, seven days a week.

I shall obey Him because I love Him, not just because it is obligatory to do so. I shall seek out ways to obey Him. I shall read and study the Scriptures to find out if there is any specific commandment that I should be obeying but that I have not obeyed thus far.

Frances Ridley Havergal, in the preface to one of her little books, wrote:

A Royal Commandment from Him!
Some of His royal commandments are made so "plain upon tables, that he may run that readeth". Some are carved between the lines of the tablets of sacred history, and flash out only as the candle of the Lord falls upon them. Some are engraved upon the gems of promise; and as we look closely into the fair colours of each jewel that the hand of faith receives, we find that it is enriched by an unerasable line of precept. But all are royal, for all are

"from Him", our King. And He has said, "If ye love Me, keep My commandments."

In a later chapter, she draws our attention to 1 Chronicles 28:8:

Keep and seek for all the commandments of the Lord your God. Is not this precept too often halved? We acknowledge our obligation to keep, but what about seeking for all the commandments of the Lord our God? Are we doing this? Even when, by His grace, we have been led to take the seven beautiful steps [in this path of obedience to His commands, mentioned] in the 119th Psalm – believing them, learning them, longing for them, loving them, delighting in them, keeping them, and not forgetting them, there remains yet this further step, *seeking for all of them*.

Do we shrink from this? Is it a bit too radical? Are we afraid of seeing something which it might be peculiarly hard to keep?

It seems [says Frances Ridley Havergal] as if it might be enough to try to keep what commandments we have seen without seeking for still more, and as if seeing more to keep would only involve us in heavier obligations and in more failures to keep them.

Then comes her further comment: "How little we must love His will if we would rather not know it lest it should clash with our own!" Does that strike a chord in our hearts? Do I think, somewhat shamefacedly, that she is digging at me?[2].

* * *

How does all this actually work out in everyday life?

When I first started Bible reading, under the guidance of the Scripture Union notes, I well remember that we were encouraged to "look for an example to follow, a warning to heed, a command to obey" every day, so that our study would not be merely a case of gathering knowledge in our heads, but be translated into practical wisdom to help us to know how to live.

James exhorts us to be "doers of the Word", and "not hearers only": "Do not merely listen to the Word," he writes, "and so deceive yourselves. Do what it says" (Jas. 1:22). In fact, James goes on to liken the person who reads and promptly forgets or ignores the practical implication of what he has read, to some short-sighted person who glances in a mirror, and immediately forgets what he looks like!

Let us look at a few Bible commands in depth, and see if we are, in fact, obeying them. What about commands with regard to our use of time? Does the Bible give us any definite guidance here? Notice what is said in Ephesians 5:15-21: "Be very careful, then, how you live – not as unwise but as wise, making the most of every opportunity ... be filled with the Spirit ... always giving thanks to God the Father for everything ..." Do I actually consider *all* my time to be important in God's service? Do I seek to use *every* opportunity to represent God's interests in the company of those around me? Am I *always* full of gratitude to God, whatever the circumstances?

How do we react to the command given us in 1 Thessalonians 5:16-18? "Be joyful always; pray continually; give thanks in all circumstances, for this is God's will for you in Christ Jesus."

Is it actually possible to be joyful always, even when everything seems to be going wrong? Can one pray continually, even in the midst of overwhelming pressures? Can one sincerely thank God in the midst of crushing sorrow?

Jesus "for the joy set before Him endured the Cross", and He can fill me with His joy at all times. If I maintain a close relationship with my Lord, and seek always to do only those things that please Him, I can pray in the midst of any situation. Whatever sorrow seeks to shatter me, I can thank God for trusting me with the experience even if I cannot understand the reason for it.

We are told in 2 Timothy 4:1,2: "In the presence of God and of Christ Jesus . . . and in view of His appearing and His kingdom, I give you this charge: Preach the Word; be prepared in season and out of season; correct, rebuke and encourage – with great patience and careful instruction." Am I living in obedience to this clear commandment? Do I so live that I could talk readily to my companions at any moment about the claims of Christ, or are there inconsistencies in my life that would make such speaking hypocritical, "conscience making cowards of us"? "In season and out of season" would seem to cover every waking moment of our lives. Our "practice" *must* be consistent with our "preaching" if others are going to be willing to listen. Not only are our lips to "correct, rebuke and encourage" others, but our lives also. How I react to each day by day irritant and aggravation, as much as the joys and pleasures, will speak more loudly and clearly than what I preach from a soap box!

Amy Carmichael, in her book called *If* emphasises the point, that my reaction to daily situations reveals to all around me whether I am full of the love of Calvary, or only full of myself. Two short quotations from that book may help to illustrate this: "If interruptions annoy me, and private cares make me impatient; if I shadow the souls about me because I myself am shadowed, then I know nothing of Calvary love." And the one I remember best: "If a sudden jar can cause me to speak an impatient, unloving word, then I know nothing of Calvary love," with a footnote: "For a cup brimful of sweet water cannot spill even one drop of bitter water however suddenly jolted"[3].

My attitude *at all times* must be Godward. My "use" of time is important in the eyes of God. I am not my own, but am bought with a price, and I must therefore work continuously for my Master's pleasure and not my own. It is so easy to think "Oh, but God wouldn't mind me enjoying this little something for a short while!" and even quoting Scripture to support my momentary desire: "Didn't He say that He had given us all good things to enjoy?" when my conscience tells me clearly that the "little something" is a waste of God's time, or even directly opposed to God's purposes, or possibly hateful to God's nature – such as watching a television programme using suggestive, or even blasphemous, language, that can do nothing at all to increase my love for God.

What about the use of "my" money and goods? Have the Scriptures anything to say about that? Are there any direct and clear commands to guide me in this matter? "Do not store up for yourselves treasures on earth, where moth and rust destroy, and where thieves break in and steal. But store up for yourselves treasures in heaven ... For where your treasure is, there your heart will be also" (Matt. 6:19-21).

That seems pretty definite, and comes directly from Christ Himself. It is not even given as a word of advice, but as an imperative command! It is of course speaking of concern for myself. It is not here saying that I am not to be thoughtful in saving for the well-being of those dependent on me; it is, however, a specific directive in the use of my goods.

Jesus told His disciples a parable which we read in Luke 12:16-21:

The ground of a certain rich man produced a good crop. He thought to himself, "What shall I do? I have no place to store my crops."

Then he said, "This is what I'll do. I will tear down my barns and build bigger ones, and there I will store all my grain and my goods. And I'll say to myself, 'You have plenty of good things laid up for many years. Take life easy; eat, drink and be merry.'"

But God said to him, "You fool! This very night your life will be demanded from you. Then who will get what you have prepared for yourself?"

This is how it will be with anyone who stores up things for himself but is not rich towards God.

Once again we get a clear directive that we may find painful and wish not to hear, and to which we would prefer not to have our attention drawn! But how do I measure up to such a standard, given me by my heavenly Master Himself?

Christ warns us again and again that worldly riches, which probably include not only money and possessions, but also public opinion and popularity, can so easily take over and dominate our lives to the exclusion of everything else.

He explained the meaning of the parable of the sower thus: "What was sown among the thorns is the man who hears the Word, but the worries of this life and the deceitfulness of wealth choke it, making it unfruitful" (Matt. 13:22).

Are we willing to be warned about our attitude to worldly wealth, and to keep "things" in perspective? Is my spiritual life and its development more important than the acquisition of possessions, material and abstract?

What about Ananias and Sapphira? They owned the money that was realised by the sale of their property, and they had the right to choose what they did with it, but they lied. They wanted to appear publicly to be extraordinarily generous. Whatever their motive – even if they were a little afraid for the future, and so kept back a bit for "a rainy day", which would be perfectly natural and permissible – they sinned in that they lied. They wanted to appear one thing when actually they were another. This is a common temptation in our day, when material possessions often seem to denote our place in the social scale. Am I obeying God's command to hold such things lightly, and to be more deeply concerned with spiritual development, and God's evaluation of my life? If He were to weigh me in the balances, would I be found wanting with regard to my attitude to goods and riches?

Another Biblical command is to pray. God gives us certain

instructions as to how to pray, when and where, and about what; and we are warned of certain conditions which will hinder our prayers being answered. Knowing that I am commanded to pray, in order to obey that command, do I deliberately set myself to fulfil all those conditions that will facilitate prayer and to avoid anything that directly impedes even a spirit of prayer? "If I had cherished sin in my heart, the Lord would not have listened" (Ps. 66:18).

If I have lied and refuse to acknowledge it, hoping to get away with it; if I have cheated or stolen or lost my temper, and refuse to confess it, trusting that with the passage of time it will be conveniently forgotten; if I am harbouring a grudge in my heart against someone who has wronged me, or seeking to justify myself in a situation where I have been maligned; if I have knowingly fallen short of God's standard in any instance and resolutely turn a blind eye to it, I *cannot* pray and expect to be heard.

Christ commanded us to pray that we might be able to resist temptation: "Watch and pray so that you will not fall into temptation. The spirit is willing, but the body is weak" (Matt. 26:41).

If I then put myself into situations where prayer is virtually impossible, how can I obey this commandment? If I sit up to all hours, perhaps watching a television or video programme, or listening to radio, or immersed in a book, or chatting with a friend, how can I give myself to a prayer fellowship with God? The body is too tired to stay awake and the mind too tired to concentrate. If I choose to read books or to go out with companions or to indulge in occupations that hinder my growth in my relationship with God, am I not deliberately disobeying this commandment?

It is fairly easy to persuade myself that a book or a companion or an occupation is in order, through which I might "witness ..." or "learn so as to be able to witness ..." or "form a bridge of friendship so as to be able to witness at a later date ..." but if it puts me in a dubious or compromising position, it cannot be of God. God never asks us to sin to achieve His purposes. God will never tempt us to evil in order to do good.

God has commanded us to be pure in thought, word and deed. His Word says: "Blessed are the pure in heart, for they will see God" (Matt. 5:8); "Keep yourself pure" (1 Tim. 5:22).

If I set myself to obey this command to be pure, I shall have to refuse to go to certain things, to watch certain programmes, to associate with certain people, to indulge in certain habits, that are a spiritual hindrance. To say that I love God and that I know I am not my own but am bought with the price of the shed blood of Christ, and yet continue to practise certain acts and to maintain certain attitudes that are diametrically opposed to God's Holiness, would make me a liar.

We are to follow the example of Christ, who "when they hurled their insults at Him, He did not retaliate; when He suffered, He made no threats. Instead, He entrusted Himself to Him who judges justly" (1 Pet. 2:23).

Am I willing to deny myself and my imagined rights – right to be considered, right to be recognised and acknowledged, right to choose – and trust God in every circumstance, even when I appear to be trodden underfoot by others, trampled on and ignored? Will I obey God, rather than my natural instinct for self-preservation? Will I trust God to vindicate me instead of leaping in to my own self-defence when falsely accused or passed over?

Am I determined to have one goal in life, that of being pleasing to God, at whatever cost to myself? Do I really desire to seek first the advancement of His concerns and His standards? Can I honestly say that I so long for others to come to know God in all His majesty and grace that I will forgo anything that would hinder them, that I will seek to do nothing that would cause them to stumble?

For none of us lives to himself alone and none of us dies to himself alone. If we live, we live to the Lord; and if we die, we die to the Lord ... Therefore let us stop passing judgment on one another. Instead, make up your mind not to put any stumbling block or obstacle in your brother's way (Rom. 14:7,8,13).

If I break the speed limits and so cause someone else to say: "And you call yourself a Christian!" I have become a "stumbling block". If I lose control of myself and become angry over some petty slight; if I drop a hint to the boss of someone else's incompetence and so gain promotion at their expense; if I promise to do something but, when the time comes, ignore that fact when I find that it is a little inconvenient; or one hundred and one other such "ifs" that could give an onlooker the right to say: "And you call yourself a Christian!" I have become a stumbling block.

God has set out His standard for us in Psalm 15:

Lord, who may dwell in Your sanctuary?
Who may live on Your holy hill?

He whose walk is blameless
and who does what is righteous,
who speaks the truth from his heart
and has no slander on his tongue,
who does his neighbour no wrong
and casts no slur on his fellow man,
who despises a vile man
but honours those who fear the Lord,
who keeps his oath
even when it hurts,
who lends his money without usury
and does not accept a bribe against the innocent.

He who does these things
will never be shaken.

Is this my standard? Am I willing to set about revealing the love of God in the world I live in by *obeying* His Word?

* * *

The spiritual process of learning obedience is frequently closely associated with *suffering* in one form or another. This "suffering" may be only anticipatory, because the very word "obedience" can conjure up today the idea of submission to another who wishes to dominate. Therefore the one giving the obedience is tempted to think that he will automatically have to give up his rights to self-expression, and so "suffer" the indignity of servitude. On the other hand, the "suffering" may be the means needed to help someone to realise that only by obedience can the reality of their love and respect for another be shown. The suffering may be physical, but more probably it will be mental or emotional, as one learns to exchange a desire to dominate for a desire to serve.

As Christians, the close link between obedience and suffering should not surprise us when we remember: "Although He was a Son, He learned obedience from what He suffered" (Heb. 5:8).

The hymn writer, George Matheson, encapsulated this paradoxical truth for us in the words:

> Make me a captive, Lord,
>   and then I shall be free;
> Force me to render up my sword,
>   and I shall conqu'ror be.

Then, speaking of his heart in a later verse, he continues:

> It cannot freely move
>   till Thou hast wrought its chain;
> Enslave it with Thy matchless love,
>   and deathless it shall reign.

Chained up firmly, yet able to move freely! Totally enslaved and stripped of all personal rights, yet reigning supreme! The paradox is such that we need to look at this truth very carefully to understand just what God is seeking to teach us.

This enslavement that liberates the soul is the embodiment of Holiness, and is only possible as the expression of love and trust. As my love for God increases, and my trust in Him deepens through the experience of His trustworthiness, so I come to see that my greatest safety lies in His protection. The more wholly I accept His ways and seek to obey His voice, the more completely can I rely on Him to protect me from all the forces that would seek to trip me up and cause me to disobey.

In a national army, a soldier who is seeking to obey his commanding officer is proud to wear the uniform of his regiment, and knows it gives him the right to fulfil his duty in certain places and circumstances where someone not entitled to wear that uniform would not be allowed entry. It will also confer on him the right to the protection of the army at all times of difficulty and danger. However, if the same soldier is abusing his position by disobedience to his commanding officer, the same uniform can be the means of bringing him to court and disciplinary action.

Jesus Himself taught that freedom comes through obeying His teaching:

To the Jews who had believed Him, Jesus said, "If you hold to my teaching, you are really My disciples. Then you will know the truth, and the truth will set you free."

They answered Him, "We are Abraham's descendants and have never been slaves of anyone. How can you say that we shall be set free?"

Jesus replied, "I tell you the truth, everyone who sins is a slave to sin. Now a slave has no permanent place in the family, but a son belongs to it for ever. So if the Son sets you free, you will be free indeed" (John 8:31–36).

Paul wrote a whole chapter in his famous letter to the Christians in Rome on this same subject, pointing out that having been freed from the slavery of Satan, we voluntarily offer ourselves as slaves to God, and so enter the freedom of His service.

He begins the sixth chapter of that letter by reminding us that as Christians, our old nature that was in us before conversion is to be "buried with Christ", united with Him in His death, so that the new nature, given to us by the Holy Spirit when we became Christians, can rise with Christ in His resurrection to live a new life. This is the whole plan of redemption encapsulated in one sentence.

The "old self", he says, is to be crucified, so that "we should no longer be slaves to sin – because anyone who has died has been freed from sin", that is, from that dominion which demands our obedience to it. "Therefore do not let sin reign in your mortal body so that you obey its evil desires ... For sin shall not be your master ..."

"Don't you know", Paul continues in his well-reasoned argument, "that when you offer yourselves to someone to obey him as slaves, you are slaves to the one whom you obey – whether you are slaves to sin, which leads to death, or to obedience, which leads to righteousness?" If we are living our daily lives in the assurance of the fact that, by the death and resurrection of Christ, we are actually living "in Him", surely therefore it is incumbent upon us to submit ourselves to God's rule?

James Philip, in his very helpful booklet, *Christian Maturity*, says that the acceptance of the need of submission to God in obedience is the major hindrance to spiritual life. He writes: "The Gospel is something that must be obeyed from the heart. And this is the great stumbling block: for we are not willing to submit ..."

The Gospels call us to obedience, not as an optional extra, but as a basic requirement for all who would follow Christ. Indeed Christian freedom from the power of sin and victory in the life of Holiness only become real in our experience as we become obedient to God's Word.

When Paul thanked God that the Roman Christians, who had been "slaves to sin", had been set free from sin and had become "slaves to righteousness", he clearly stated that this transformation had not come about by a mental assent to doctrine but by wholehearted obedience to the "form of teaching" that they had received. "Thanks be to God" he writes, "that, though you used to be slaves to sin, you wholeheartedly obeyed the *form* of teaching to which you were entrusted" (Rom. 6:17) (my italics).

James Philip, in the booklet to which I referred, tells us that that word "form" (the sum of the teaching to which we are to give careful obedience if we would be holy) is the translation of a Greek word, *typos*, which literally means the "impress a die makes on a soft surface, or the mould into which molten metal is poured, and which gives shape to the metal when it is cooled". He goes on to suggest that the mould of Biblical teaching on sanctification is that of a cross. "If lives are to be sanctified", he comments, "the marks of the cross will be reproduced in them." Surely that is what is meant when we are told to deny ourselves daily, and take up the Cross and follow Christ.

He concludes this passage by saying: "It is precisely because this moral challenge is involved in the New Testament conception of faith that all the classical expressions of consecration and discipleship are given in terms of sacrifice and the note of suffering stressed."

Paul continued his treatise to the Christians in Rome by restating that we are liberated from Satan's slavery to sin in order to become God's slaves to Holiness:

> You have been set free from sin and have become slaves to righteousness ... leading to Holiness. When you were slaves to sin, you were free from the control of righteousness ... But now that you have been set free from sin and have become slaves to God, the benefit you reap leads to Holiness, and the result is eternal life (Rom. 6:18–22).

It is in the *obedience* that we offer to the teaching of God in His Word, that we prove that our faith is real and experience the enduement of the Holy Spirit for service.

But where does suffering come in? Why should this obedience that leads to liberty and freedom appear to cost so much to attain that we think of the price as suffering?

To quote James Philip again: "It is here that the crux of the whole matter lies, for, deep down, we do not really wish to *obey* in this total sense. We do not really want to die – we want to live 'for ourselves'"[4].

Obedience is a *discipline*, a deliberate, considered course of action, to bring us into line with God's will. I determine, with the help of God's Holy Spirit, to live a life that pleases Him in every detail. This demands, as a natural corollary, that I deliberately determine to give up all that displeases God. This must be an essential part of the discipline, as we have already seen in Paul's instructions to Titus:

> For the grace of God ... teaches us to say "No" to ungodliness [all that displeases God] and worldly passions [all that is controlled by worldly pressures, with no reference to God], and to live [that is, say "Yes" to] self-controlled, upright and godly lives [all that pleases God] in this present age (Titus 2:11,12).

It is this deliberate refusal to act in accordance with the world's accepted standards when these are in opposition to God's revealed standards that leads to my being different from others. Am I willing for this? Am I willing to be criticised, or laughed at, or to be ignored or despised? This is where the "suffering" comes in for most of us.

We want to be popular, liked, thought well of, accepted. This is the natural ego asserting itself. The reverse seems painful. The contemplation of the possibility of being unpopular or unaccepted by "our set" is painful. The fear of being left out of activities, of being lonely, or of not being thought well of, all this is painful – and we "suffer".

That God is offering us something far more wonderful and

lasting and real than worldly acceptance is hard to comprehend. We know those around us: we can feel their acceptance or non-acceptance. God's friendship is somehow not so easy to grasp. We are afraid that we shall "suffer loss" by exchanging the world's friendship for God's. We are not quite sure that what we shall gain will outweigh what we shall lose.

First-century Christians went through all these fears and anxieties, and Paul had to write and reassure them over and over again. Listen to him talking to the struggling young church in Corinth, telling them of his own sufferings:

Therefore we do not lose heart. Though outwardly we are wasting away, yet inwardly we are being renewed day by day. For our light and momentary troubles are achieving for us an eternal glory that far outweighs them all. So we fix our eyes not on what is seen, but on what is unseen. For what is seen is temporary, but what is unseen is eternal (2 Cor. 4:16–18).

God, through Paul and other New Testament writers, clearly tells us that as Christians we must expect trials and tribulations, usually as the world's reaction against us, as we take a stand to obey God rather than men: "Everyone who wants to live a godly life in Christ Jesus *will* be persecuted" (2 Tim. 3:12) (my italics).

James writes the same thing to the young Christian converts scattered throughout Asia Minor. It is almost the first thing they hear when they come to Christ as Saviour and join the small group of hated Christians in their town or village: "Consider it pure joy, my brothers, whenever you face trials of many kinds, because you know that the testing of your faith develops perseverance" (Jas. 1:2,3).

This *discipline* of learning to obey God rather than man, seeking to please God rather than man, may indeed seem painful at times. We may sense that we are being called upon to "suffer". Again the writer to the scattered Hebrew

Christians addressed himself to this problem:

You have forgotten that word of encouragement that addresses you as sons:

"My son, do not make light of the Lord's discipline,
and do not lose heart when He rebukes you,
because the Lord disciplines those He loves,
and He punishes everyone He accepts as a son."

Endure hardship as a discipline; God is treating you as sons. For what son is not disciplined by his father?... God disciplines us for our good, that we may share in His Holiness. No discipline seems pleasant at the time, but painful. Later on, however, it produces a harvest of righteousness and peace for those who have been trained by it (Heb. 12:5–11).

This discipline is as the fire of the kiln that hardens soft clay into porcelain, making the earthen vessel able to do the task for which it was created.

I had two good friends in Africa who taught me this lesson most vividly.

Mark Anesadze and his wife Eleanor were a young couple with two small children, who had been deeply blessed by God in the revival at Wamba. Mark particularly had a radiant face, with a great, beaming smile. He was full of warmth and loving kindness and generosity. The couple had entered the Ibambi Bible School fifteen months after I had, and they had a home on the opposite side of the compound from mine. Except for the early morning devotional hour, we went to different classes, so I did not see much of them, until I was called urgently one day.

"Nyoka! Nyoka!" rang out over the compound – "Snake! Snake!"

Their four-year-old son, Paul, had been bitten, and despite all we could do, he died the same day. I spent the night in their home, just sitting, holding Eleanor's hand. Others of their tribe from the school squatted round the room and quietly sang hymns through the long hours of darkness, and until the child was buried the next day. This drew us very close together, and a real friendship sprang up between us.

During their last year in Bible School, they were part of a team of students who came for a ten-day mission to Nebobongo, where I was then working. Through them, God ministered revival to our growing family. Students and pupils, workmen and their wives, children and hospital patients, all came under the gracious movement of the Spirit. Sins were confessed, restitution made; joy became real, and singing replaced grumbling.

Yet, in the midst of all the rejoicing, there was a heavy sorrow in their hearts. Mark and Eleanor asked me to look at their little bright three-year-old, Mary. I felt a terrible load crushing me as I diagnosed a rapidly growing cancerous growth behind her right eye.

The parents were wonderful. When I explained to them as best I could that the only possible hope was immediate surgery, and that even this would probably only offer temporary relief, after the first awful shock, they rose with quiet dignity to accept the verdict from God's hands.

"We know our loving heavenly Father cannot do ill to us or our children," they said, "and He will not let us suffer beyond what He enables us to bear."

I went with Mary to a Government hospital many miles away, and assisted the surgeon: but the growth was already far too extensive and invasive. I had to watch with the parents during the next two years as it spread to the second eye. Mary never complained. She was a lovely child, with a quiet, thoughtful face, slowly and inexorably being physically disfigured, and yet gaining steadily and surely a rare spiritual beauty.

A baby brother was born, and Mary delighted to sit and watch little Joseph, while Eleanor was in class or working in the food gardens. Mary was puzzled that Joseph did not seem to respond to her, and her parents tried to explain to her that such a young baby could not yet understand.

"But, Mummy," exclaimed Mary, "Yoani, who was born the same day as Joseph, he sits up now: and when I tickle him, he gurgles and his eyes all screw up with happiness!" The child had touched a core of uneasiness deep in Eleanor's heart. The next weekend, the parents trudged the seven miles to Nebobongo, carrying a placid, unresisting five-month-old Joseph, and accompanied by Mary, skipping along beside them, picking flowers from the banks. They watched her, with hearts hurt with hidden grief, wondering how much longer she would be with them; and neither of them looked at the still, unchanging face of the little boy, except by covert glances, too afraid to voice, even to each other, the growing dread.

It seemed beyond possibility. I was so stunned, I could not even question God's intention. Paul, the first born, was dead. Mary was dying. And now, Joseph lay there, a helpless living cripple. I suppose I played for time before telling them what I feared, but I had to be sure. I took the baby to a Government hospital for radiological investigation. But I already knew the truth. Little Joseph was never going to sit up, or smile, or talk, or in any wise relate to the family. He was a helpless, yet living, cripple. I was surprised that he had even suckled and grown so well during those first five months, but I was sure that feeding in the future would be increasingly difficult.

Once again, the parents rose to the well-nigh impossible situation, accepting that God had entrusted this helpless infant to their loving care, and they poured their affection on him, resolutely refusing to lose faith in the love of God, as some would surely have been tempted to do.

They completed their Bible School training, and were sent for a year to work under the pastor's supervision at the big district church at Wamba. After this probationary period, they were appointed to an "outchurch", in a small heathen village, full of witchcraft and pagan rites, thirty miles further east. From the outset, the villagers made it abundantly clear that the evangelist and his wife were not welcome, nor was the Gospel message of salvation they had come to share.

It was a very dark period for them. They were pioneering, in the most basic sense of the word. They had to build themselves a home in the midst of that hostile crowd; carve out a food garden from the surrounding forest with none of the usual village camaraderie; testify to the love of God by their actions, for none would listen to their words. They were ostracised. They were lonely. They were a long way from their own families or the warmth of Christian fellowship. They were "despised and rejected". Like their Saviour? It had been relatively easy in Bible School to say "Yes, Lord, we are willing" but now, could they bear it?

I planned to spend a weekend with them before leaving for furlough in July 1958, and I was looking forward to this immensely. On the Friday evening, as darkness was falling, I and three African para-medical workers made our way down the hill east of Wamba to the small village where Mark and Eleanor lived, greatly relieved that another week of clinics was safely and successfully behind us. We were tired and dirty, looking forward to the usual warm welcome, buckets of hot water, evening prayers and early bed.

As Mark and Eleanor came out of their home to welcome us, I sensed at once that there was something amiss. They were subdued, and yet somehow, there was an undercurrent of excitement. We all piled out, took our bed-rolls into the house, and then, as the boys picked up a bucket of water each to go to wash, the evangelist and his wife invited Suzanne and myself to join them on the verandah. As we sat down, in the cool of the evening, relaxing, looking up into a star-lit sky, the two shared with us an amazing story of the past few days.

They had been looking forward so much to our arrival: they wanted everything perfect to welcome us. Eleanor had freshly laundered the children's clothes and laid them out on the grass roof of their home to dry. In the back yard, they had a chicken, fattening. In their garden, they had ripening pineapples and green vegetables. Mark had just finished building a small chapel, whitewashing its mud walls and placing tree trunks in rows for benches.

On Thursday morning, Mark set off to the local river to fish. Eleanor, carrying two-year-old Joseph in a sling across her back, with five-year-old Mary carrying the new month-old baby Fibi, had gone down the steep pathway to their food garden to collect pineapples and greens. Then everything seemed to happen at once.

"You've never seen such a mess," exploded Eleanor. "The garden was destroyed: just hacked down. Not even stolen. Senseless vandalism. Devastation all around. I simply gazed at it, thunderstruck. At first, I couldn't think: I couldn't take it in. I felt rising bitterness against whoever could have been so mean."

She turned to climb back up the narrow winding trail, tears stinging her eyes, when she heard ... smelt ... sensed something awfully wrong.

"Panic caught me," she continued. "We hurried up to the village, as fast as we could."

The small chapel, only just finished and whitewashed, the pride of the last few weeks, and to be dedicated that weekend, was ablaze. Flames – smoke – smell poured out from it. Numbed and fearful, Eleanor laid Joseph down at the edge of the clearing. Snatching baby Fibi, she sent Mary to run for her father. Almost dropping Fibi beside Joseph, Eleanor began to drag away anything salvageable. She grabbed a bucket of water and threw it into the gap between the chapel and their home.

"I prayed God, the wind wouldn't turn," she remembered. "I was crying, and the tears, mingled with smoke, burned my eyes. Sparks were flying in every direction, and I was frantic for Mark's help."

"Yes," he took over quietly. "Our wee Mary came flying down, shouting and crying incoherently. I gathered her up in

my arms and hurried back to the scene of destruction."
Mary ran over to the other two children, squatting beside
them and drawing them back into the shade of the trees,
away from the sparks and the heat of the fire. With eyes
round with horror, she watched her parents frantically
pulling the burning grass off the chapel roof, trampling it
underfoot to stop the holocaust spreading. With burnt
hands and feet, and eyes streaming from the stinging smoke,
they got the fire under control at last – but there was nothing
left of the chapel except a charred shell.

"As I worked," Mark remarked, "I suppose I registered
that no one was helping us."

That is so unlike the African. Whatever their differences,
when tragedy strikes, everyone moves in to help. One would
have expected the whole village to have rushed to their aid.
No. On the contrary, sullen and derisive, they had stood in
their doorways and watched.

Puzzled, Mark added "They all seemed to hate us ..."

"That's it," chipped in Eleanor. "Ever since we came here,
to bring them the Gospel of love and peace, they have hated
us and determined to drive us away."

When the fire had died down, they had found other
damage inflicted against them. Their one chicken was gone.
The children's clothes, drying on the thatch, were gone.

"A great bitterness welled up inside me," Eleanor
conceded. "I just felt I hated them all." Humbly she
confessed, "I almost turned on God, with a deep inner cry:
'Why? Why? Why have You let all this happen to us? Why
didn't You stop them? Aren't we serving You? Haven't we
given up everything else to be here as Your representatives?'"

I thought back to Paul's death at Bible School; Mary with
cancer behind her eyes; Joseph a helpless cripple ... and I
was tempted to think they had suffered enough. Sensing my
thoughts, Eleanor added, "And my brother, an unconverted
pagan man, is a wealthy shopkeeper with two wives and
several healthy children!"

Mark and Eleanor had cleared up the mess and debris in

silence, with a barrier between them. Mark's big heart of love could reach through the darkness and touch God, and know "that in all things God works for the good of those who *love* Him" (Rom. 8:28), but he could not reach through the barrier to help Eleanor in her bitterness.

In the evening, the children in bed, they had sat together on the verandah. Mark had taken up his Bible to read aloud as usual, but Eleanor shut her heart, she told me, unwilling to hear the words.

"I didn't want to be helped. I was bitter and hurt, and couldn't see why I shouldn't be. I knew if we prayed, I'd have to change, and quite honestly, I didn't want to change. Why shouldn't I be bitter? Hadn't I suffered enough?"

"Then I seemed to doze," she continued, "even while Mark was praying. And I saw four large earthen jars – you know, the ordinary kind we all use in our homes. They faded . . . and I jerked myself awake, and wondered vaguely why I had imagined them. They just had no connection with anything else at that particular time."

She went on to say how this had been repeated, just as the first time. She paused, and her eyes filled with tears, and a smile played at the corner of her lips.

"A third time," she whispered, "just the same, only now a Voice spoke, telling me to go near and look closely. And I saw the jars were filled with water. Then as I looked, the level of water began to fall ... A trickle snaked across the verandah ... I stretched out a hand, and touched the jar ..." She paused, with a deep breath, obviously re-living the moment. Shaking herself, she concluded, "The vision faded and I woke."

"Yes," interrupted Mark with a laugh. "She started up, grabbed my arm and almost shouted at me to stop praying!"

"I just had to share," she explained apologetically.

They had discussed together what she had seen, puzzled as to its implication when suddenly Eleanor had realised what God was saying.

"The jar was *soft*," she murmured. "Soft ... unfired ..."

So the jars were useless to fulfil the job for which they were made. They were made from the right earth, well matured, well rolled, well moulded – but "soft". They had not yet been fired in the kiln.

As they shared this testimony with me, my eyes filled with tears. It was all too poignant and I ached for them. I could only see all they had suffered; but as we sat and chatted together, they showed me what the Lord was saying to them.

"It isn't really suffering, is it?" Eleanor explained. "God has merely offered us the privilege of being made more like our Saviour, stripped of everything that is unlike Him, or unhelpful to our testimony, or unnecessary for the ministry that He has planned for us. Even when He took Paul home, though it was terribly hard to accept at the time, He told us that He was teaching us to accept His comfort so that we could comfort others in like circumstances."

Mark interjected: "It isn't too bad when the training and discipline only hurts ourselves, but it isn't so easy to see the children suffer too. Sometimes, we haven't had enough food for them, nor money to buy clothes for them, and then it has seemed hard. Yet the Lord has taught us to hold all our possessions lightly. He didn't even have a place to sleep, did He?"

"We so long to be available to God, so that He can use us to help others," they continued. "And yet there seem so many lessons to learn and we are slow. I think we have seen that the most important thing He is saying to us is to *obey* Him in everything, and to trust Him to work out the consequences. We don't have to reason it all out or understand why He does some things – we just have to trust and obey."

We knelt together later that evening, and as Mark and Eleanor poured their hearts out to God in childlike confidence in His goodness, I just wanted to whisper: "Dear God, forgive me! I've rebelled at Your ways in my life; I've argued with You and wanted my own way. I've disobeyed so often. Can You forgive me? I want to say, 'Not my will, but

Yours, be done', but I'm afraid. I want to ask you to fire me, in the kiln of Your love, and make me into a vessel capable of fulfilling Your purposes – but I'm scared at what it may cost, how much it may hurt. Please make me willing to be made willing for the discipline of total obedience to Your every known command."

The Master Potter has chosen us, and taken us into His nail-pierced hands, to mould us as clay into the vessels He has planned. He is patiently working on each "lump of clay", ridding it of all impurities, removing every tiny bit of grit that would spoil the beauty of the finished jar. He alone knows how to fire His jar, in what kiln and at what temperature, that it may become "holy, useful to the Master and prepared to do any good work" (2 Tim. 2:21), that He may entrust it to carry about His Treasure: "We have this treasure in jars of clay to show that this all-surpassing power is from God and not from us" (2 Cor. 4:7).

5

Fourth step – Service

Holiness and Service.

If a man therefore purge himself from these, he shall be a vessel unto honour, sanctified, and meet for the Master's use, and prepared unto every good work (2 Tim. 2:21)(AV).

Through the whole of Scripture we have seen that whatever God sanctifies is to be used in the service of His Holiness. His Holiness is an infinite energy that only finds its rest in making holy: to the revelation of what He is in Himself, "I the Lord am holy," God continually adds the declaration of what He does, "I am the Lord that makes holy." Whatever we read of as holy, was taken into the service of the Holiness of God.

Of Israel, whom God redeemed from Egypt that they might be a holy nation, God said, "Let my people go, that they may serve Me."

Can it be thought possible ... that now Holiness and service would be put asunder? Impossible! Here first we shall fully realise how essential they are to each other ... We are only made holy that we may serve. We can only serve as we are holy. Holiness is essential to effectual service.

A vessel of honour, one whom the King will

delight to honour, must be a vessel cleansed from all defilement of the flesh and the spirit. Then only can it be a sanctified vessel, possessed and in-dwelt by God's Holy Spirit. So it becomes meet for the Master's use.

Yes, Holiness is essential to effectual service. And service is no less essential to true Holiness.

Let your whole life be one distinctly and definitely given up to God for His use and service. Your circumstances may appear to be unfavourable. God may appear to keep the door closed against your working for Him in the way you would wish; your sense of unfitness may be painful. Still, let it be a matter settled between God and the soul, that your longing for Holiness is that you may be fitter for Him to use.

Revd Andrew Murray[1].

5 Fourth step – Service

"Can you boil a potato in a candlestick?"

* * *

The preacher pronounced his text clearly, and repeated it slowly for emphasis: "The glorious riches of this mystery: . . . Christ in you, the hope of glory" (Col. 1:27). The school hall in Nairobi was warm and crowded for the fourth conference address at the annual Kenya Keswick Convention. My eyes roved over the congregation, and saw with pleasure the number of national delegates. Many of the missionaries, I noticed, looked tired and thin, and yet I could not help but notice how eagerly they were listening, hungry for encouragement and for renewal of vision to continue their demanding tasks.

I was making a great effort to stay awake in the increasing heat, when I heard these words: "Can you boil a potato in a candlestick?"

I was suddenly wide awake, leaning forward in amazement. Had I really heard the preacher ask that question, or had I just imagined it?

"Well, can you?" I reasoned. "How stupid! Of course not!" But what was the inference? Why ask the question? Where, oh where was the connection with the text?

As one of the four people asked to speak on the year's text, I had been studying it for six months. We were, in turn, to emphasise Christ in us, hating sin; Christ in us, loving God; Christ in us, obeying His will; and Christ in us, serving others. In preparation for the conference, I had sought to understand each of these four aspects of the truth of the text – "Christ in you, the hope of glory" – in order to present the third aspect in relationship to the other three. The text had begun to take hold of me, so no wonder I was startled by this extraordinary phrase – "Can you boil a potato in a candlestick?" – wondering how on earth it could relate to the subject in hand. It seemed to have no bearing on the subject and was so wholly unexpected.

I'm not sure now that I ever worked out the relevance of the phrase to the text under discussion, but over the years, I have frequently returned to it with a wry sense of humour.

How frequently our lives are spoiled by an attitude of "if only ..." "If only I were a saucepan instead of a candlestick ... how much easier it would be to be useful to God!"

"If only I had his qualifications or her gifts ... If only I lived in a different community or had a more satisfying job ... If only I had not made that mistake years ago or missed that opportunity last week ... how different might my life now be!"

Others of us may look out on the suffering world around us and be tempted to sigh, "If only God would raise up another John Wesley ..." thinking that thus the masses might be reached with the Gospel of Redemption. I believe it was Watchman Nee who said that if God had wanted another John Wesley, He could easily have sent one! But He has not. He has sent you and me instead. And God knows His business: He does not make mistakes. If He wanted to boil a potato, He could send a saucepan! But if He wants to send the Light of Life to a needy world in its darkness, it is more reasonable to suppose that He will send a candlestick. And if God wants a candlestick of a certain size and colour, to carry a particular Candle to a particular dark spot, He can doubtless make that candlestick exactly as He wants it.

I believe that is what He is busy doing with each one of us, His children – making or re-making each one of us into a candlestick that is according to the perfect pattern He has planned:

For He chose us in Him [Christ] before the creation of the world to be holy and blameless in His sight (Eph. 1:4). For we are God's workmanship, created in Christ Jesus to do good works, which God prepared in advance for us to do (Eph. 2:10).

God's business is creating and moulding candlesticks to carry brightly burning Candles into places of darkness. Am I willing to be moulded into one of God's candlesticks, rather than saucepans? Am I willing to be made to fit a particular Candle, rather than demanding that God shapes the Candle to fit the candlestick? Am I prepared for God to prescribe the way I carry the Candle, rather than demanding my right to do so in the way I choose? Am I content that God should send me and my Candle into any dark spot that He chooses, without first asking my permission?

How patient God is, in the fulfilment of His strategy. I can look back now and marvel at His gracious dealing to prepare me for the job He had planned for me at Nyankunde. I am at heart a teacher, yet, for twelve years, God kept me at work in general medicine at Nebobongo. Often I was tempted to grumble and to ask, "Why, God?"

In 1966, following the great destruction caused by the rebellion in north-east Zaire, God sent me to help in the re-opening of medical services at Nyankunde. My part in the team for that inter-mission medical project was to be the training of national para-medical personnel – teaching! At that time, the newly appointed Minister of Health in the Kinshasa Government determined that only fully qualified doctors, with at least ten years' experience of medical practice in the country, would be eligible as directors of colleges for the training of national para-medical personnel.

In 1953, God had known that that decree would be passed in 1966, and He had patiently shaped a particular candlestick to carry the Candle in that particular spot at that particular moment in time. I may not have rejoiced in the training process, but I certainly learned that God never makes mistakes. We can trust Him absolutely and always. God wants to fit us perfectly into His plan, if we will allow Him to do so. He is willing to bring all circumstances to bear to that end. Ephesians 2:10 tells us that God had already prepared, "before the creation of the world", the "good works" that He wants us to do, when He planned our salvation. He doesn't have to look around to see if He can find a job to fit my qualifications when I decide to apply to Him for employment! No. All is prepared. The only problem is my unwillingness to obey and take my part in the predetermined plan.

Look at Jonah. During the reign of Jeroboam II, somewhere between 793 and 753 BC, maybe fifty years before the fall of the northern kingdom of Israel, Jonah was born to Amittai in Gath Hepher, a few miles north of Nazareth in Galilee. He grew up in the knowledge of God.

The times in which he lived were not dissimilar to our own. To a large extent, men ignored God and went their own ways. Few acknowledged any absolute standards of righteousness. Idolatry abounded on all sides. Permissiveness was the order of the day, harlotry acceptable and evil considered right. To be godly in such a society was to be "peculiar" and to stick out like a sore thumb.

And there was Nineveh. Just to say the name of that city brought a reaction of hatred and of fear. The name summed up for the Israelite all that was most evil and sinister. It was a vast conglomerate of four cities, with a population of over two million, covering four hills and the intervening valleys. It was so wide flung that it would take three days to walk round the perimeter wall of this great capital of the heathen empire of Assyria. Legends were rife about the evil practised within its walls, and of the barbaric cruelty meted out to its subjugated peoples.

Not only did the Israelites hate the vice and savagery of the Ninevites, but they feared lest they too might eventually fall to the mighty army and suffer the same dehumanising wickedness as other neighbouring territories had done. Yes,

"Nineveh" was equated with "enemy"; and since the iron dictator, Pul, the descendant of Tiglath-Pileser III, had seized the throne, the ruthless tyranny had only increased the depth of hatred and fear in the hearts of all the surrounding nations.

At this moment, God spoke to Jonah. "Go to ... Nineveh and preach against it ..."

God was preparing a candlestick to carry His Candle into a very dark area at that precise moment in history – but the candlestick wasn't willing for the task. In fact, Jonah could not believe his ears. It was impossible – absolutely, totally impossible. God just could not mean it. Go to Nineveh? "Dear God, anywhere but not there!" No one would ever believe that God had sent him. He would be blacklisted, turned out by his own people. No one would support him. And deep down inside, though he did not say so, not even to himself, Jonah was scared stiff! No, God, no! Not that.

"And anyway, if I did do anything so outlandishly foolish," Jonah may have reasoned with himself, "what on earth would I say to the Ninevites? They are good for nothing except extermination, to be wiped off the face of the earth. Oh, I know, You could tell me to warn them of judgment to come, and to talk to them about Your holy wrath against their abominable sins, but God, I also know that, in the end, Your mercy would prevail ... and for *me* to be seen by my fellow Jews as a messenger of mercy and forgiveness and light to our arch enemy ... No! Please God, no."

So Jonah fled.

Is not the situation today very similar? How many "candlesticks" argue with their Creator when He seeks to direct them to an apparently unsalubrious spot or to a hard and unresponsive people? How many are even willing to be candlesticks, preferring rather to be saucepans?

A young Christian, who has been brought under conviction of sin by the Holy Spirit and to a state of true repentance and regeneration, is filled with a deep love for the

Saviour who died as his Substitute. He is determined to
show that love in a life of service, but suddenly realises that
God is sending him out into the world of today to live a *holy*
life. His heart shrinks within him as he contemplates the
implications. Does God not understand just how sinful and
wicked and immoral the world is today? It is surely
impossible to stay clean in such a polluted atmosphere. And
anyway, how could one holy life affect the vast torrent of
unholiness all around? It would be like putting one tiny
candle in a vast, unlit cathedral and expecting its light to
expel the darkness!

So the Christian is tempted to turn tail and flee: maybe
back into a local fellowship or small group of like-minded
people: maybe, as Jonah, to go in the opposite direction –
anywhere except where God is pointing.

What has gone wrong with the love that wanted to serve?

Is it perhaps that the motive that prompted the service was
inadequate? If "I" want to show God how much I love Him,
by giving all I've got to serve Him, whatsoever it may mean
and wheresoever it may be, it is quite possible that this
service may not be according to God's predetermined plan.
"I" may find myself a potato trying to shine in a candlestick!
The "I" is in the way. The motive is self-something: maybe
self-gratification, self-satisfaction, or any of what A. W.
Tozer calls "the hyphenated sins of the self-life". I am
seeking to prove to myself that I am what I hope I am, or that
I love whom I hope I love. This type of motivation is
insufficient: it does not work.

Hatred of sin and love for the Saviour must lead, first and
foremost, to obedience. Obedience to the Word of God will
show itself in service. Because I love Him, I delight to obey
Him; because I obey Him, I delight to serve Him. This will be
true godly service, a giving without any thought of gaining.

I beseech you, therefore, brethren, by the mercies of God,
that ye present your bodies a living sacrifice, holy,
acceptable unto God, which is your reasonable service.

And be not conformed to this world: but be ye transformed by the renewing of your mind, that ye may prove what is that good, and acceptable, and perfect, will of God" (Rom. 12:1,2)(AV).

"Reasonable service" is translated in newer versions as "spiritual worship". To be acceptable to God, both service and worship must be holy and in obedience to His command that we should offer ourselves as "living sacrifices". Christ died on the Cross as our vicarious sacrifice. Not only must there have been a decisive act in the past when I committed my life to Christ, being identified with Him in His death, but there must also be a continual daily identifying of myself with that death, in putting aside my own will and self-pleasing, in order to live according to His will and good pleasure. This is the deliberate daily choosing to "die" to self, in order to allow the Spirit of Christ to in-dwell me and to rule my choices, so that I can say with Paul: "I have been crucified with Christ and I no longer live, but Christ lives in me. The life I live in the body, I live by faith in the Son of God, who loved me and gave Himself for me" (Gal. 2:20).

The writer to the Hebrews says: "Let us have grace, whereby we may serve God acceptably with reverence and godly fear: for our God is a consuming fire" (Heb. 12:28,29) (AV). Expounding this verse, the New Bible Commentary puts it very clearly: "Let us appropriate the grace so abundantly available to serve God in ways well pleasing in His sight, i.e. to offer to God acceptable worship. In the presence of such a God and in the face of such a prospect this will be with a real sense of unworthiness and awe. Only those who thus follow after Holiness will survive His judgment, see the Lord, and reign eternally with Him"[2].

* * *

Let us look again at Jonah, and see what he did next.

He had no idea that God could ever use the wicked and

hated Assyrians as His rod of judgment against Israel. All Jonah could see was the impossibility of the situation in which he found himself.

"Surely God does not mean me to go and offer Salvation to that brutal city of Nineveh?" was his natural reasoning.

Oh, yes, Jonah acknowledged God, acknowledged that He was the One unique Creator of earth and sea; and he wanted to serve God to show his allegiance, but ... he was determined that *he* would choose how and where! Jonah was not yet so in love with God that obedience to His voice was an essential corollary, from which would flow God-directed service. He was not yet willing to be thought "peculiar", nor to become the laughing stock of his own people: so he ran away from God's command and from the responsibility of obedience.

Is God really expecting us to reveal, by holy living, true godliness in the midst of the ungodliness that reigns in our world today? Would we not be like tiny candles in an ocean of darkness? Does He really expect every Christian "to say 'No' to ungodliness and worldly passions, and to live self-controlled, upright and godly lives in this present age" (Titus 2:12,13)? Jonah was scared stiff to face Nineveh; are we as scared to face our world?

Not only have we to be willing that God should mould us into His candlesticks for the individual jobs He has planned for us, but also we must be willing to do that prepared job in the way prescribed by God. Rightly to fulfil our designated task, we shall need instruction in the procedure to be adopted.

Some perhaps are tempted to ask if God's standards for service are really practicable in the twentieth century. Is it not necessary for us to re-think the procedure and re-word the instructions to suit today's culture in the light of today's corruption? Should we not contextualise the Scripture to fit in with modern thought? Such a verse as is found in Micah 6:8 –

He has showed you, O man, what is good.
And what does the Lord require of you?
To act justly and to love mercy
and to walk humbly with your God.

– sounds so simple, but it just does not seem to fit in with the contemporary scene – or does it?

Firstly, *"to act justly"*. God is speaking. To understand what He means we must think as He thinks and judge whether our actions are just or not, by using the yardstick of His justice. We must acknowledge His right to determine the standards by which He will judge us and our actions. Of course, this is a tremendous challenge in an age that has slipped into an acceptance of "situational ethics" and a tacit agreement that there are no such things as "absolute standards". Today it is widely believed that standards must depend on culture, education, opportunities, economics, any or all of which can change from place to place, and from time to time.

We are being quietly yet steadily brain-washed into believing that Christianity is wrong, even that God's ways are actually unethical, and certainly that Holiness, as God describes it, is totally impracticable. For example, to maintain a standard of "giving service" in a climate of "getting advantage" may cause mockery and raised eyebrows. If we were to persist in such a stand, it could lead to a failure to receive deserved promotion.

A gentle hint that a little more pressure by a salesman, with a slightly decreased emphasis on truth, might well gain a needed promotion and increased salary. Given quietly at a moment of known need or family hardship, such a hint can be very difficult to resist; especially as "everyone else does it", and one's peers are leaving one behind in the proverbial rat-race. At that moment, to be able to detach oneself from the actual situation, to weigh up and consider impartially the underlying principles, and then to be true to one's convictions and stand for what one believes to be right, can be incredibly difficult.

To keep one's word even when this may be injurious to one's apparent interests; to be utterly loyal, when one might gain promotion by a little subtle gossip; to be honestly content, when a propitious hint could better one's lot; ... these are standards of service that God laid before us when David wrote Psalm 15, as we saw in a previous chapter.

This is God's prescribed standard of procedure. All my activities, public and private, must be "just" according to this standard, because "I am not my own". Christ has bought me with the price paid at Calvary. As His, I am to "mirror" Him, that others shall see Him in me. I am to act always and only as He would in each situation and under all circumstances.

The New Testament gives us very positive statements as to how to "act justly". Paul, in his letter to the Ephesian church, enjoined the young Christians to godly service in their community: "It was He who gave some to be apostles, some to be prophets, some to be evangelists, and some to be pastors and teachers, to prepare God's people for *works of service*, so that the body of Christ may be built up..." (Eph. 4:11,12) (my italics).

He then went on to remind them that, to serve in a way pleasing to God, they must first put off their old, corrupt self, and then put on the new self "created to be like God in true righteousness and Holiness". He then detailed to them how this new nature would act, linking a negative demand to reject unjust behaviour and to shun expediency with a positive command to practise goodness, both in obedience to God and in service to one another. As we read in Ephesians 4:25–32:

> Therefore each of you must put off falsehood and speak truthfully to his neighbour, for we are all members of one body. "In your anger do not sin": Do not let the sun go down while you are still angry ... He who has been stealing must steal no longer, but must work, doing something useful with his own hands, that he may have

something to share with those in need.
Do not let any unwholesome talk come out of your mouths, but only what is helpful for building others up according to their needs, that it may benefit those who listen. And do not grieve the Holy Spirit of God, with whom you were sealed for the day of redemption. Get rid of all bitterness, rage and anger, brawling and slander, along with every form of malice. Be kind and compassionate to one another, forgiving each other, just as in Christ God forgave you.

Christian service is the overflow of superabounding devotion to God, as Oswald Chambers puts it: "God gets me into a relationship with Himself whereby I understand His call, then I do things out of sheer love for Him on my own account. To serve God is the deliberate love-gift of a nature that has heard the call of God"[3]. But for that service of love to be acceptable to God it must be in accord with God's explicit commands. If, in serving, I lie to promote my own ends or increase my profitability, that service becomes unacceptable to God. If I blast off in anger at a colleague or at an employee, and fail to apologise for my loss of self-control, my service ceases to be acceptable.

If I allow myself to "fiddle" the books or make a knowingly false entry, for whatever purpose; if I join in conversation that is unseemly, laugh at jokes that are questionable, listen to language that dishonours the God I seek to serve; if I speak or act in any way to defraud another, out of malice or spite or revenge; if in any degree I cease to be kindly and considerate of others, I make my service unacceptable in the eyes of God.

To "act justly" in such a manner as Paul has detailed here is the only way for a Christian to know peace – peace with God, peace with himself, peace with his fellow men. It is the only way for a society to live together in harmony and prosperity. All the ills of society today are the result of a refusal to acknowledge God's right to declare what is just and to set absolute standards for our behaviour. Is the selfishness that dominates our culture today not the result of each one wanting his own way, and setting up his own right to determine what is just? This reminds us of the state of affairs in the days of the Judges in the Old Testament: "In those days Israel had no king; everyone did as he saw fit" (Judg. 21:25).

To *act justly* is the way that God has planned for us to live, in order to achieve His purpose and to fulfil His will. It is the appointed way to "serve God acceptably", and to show forth the Holiness that the Spirit is creating in us.

This Holiness will reveal itself also in a God-given desire to *love mercy*. We shall seek always to lift those who are down, to encourage those who are discouraged, to help those in need. We shall be willing to think the best of another, rather than the worst; to be grieved when another fails, rather than to rejoice in his downfall; to pray rather than to gossip.

This Holiness will enable us to "*walk humbly*" with our God – as the New Bible Commentary says, "in utter dependence upon His enablement to lead a godly life, and in full recognition of the total lack of personal ability or merit which might furnish a base for pride or self-justification"[2].

To walk humbly with God we need to be transformed into His image by the Holy Spirit and this is achieved by deliberate obedience to all He reveals to us. We must give Him *all* that we are and have. There has to be a *total* surrender and *absolute* submission of our will to His, a true echoing of the prayer of the Saviour in the Garden of Gethsemane: "Not as I will, but as you will" (Matt. 26:39).

When, in prayer, we look at ourselves honestly and recognise our poverty of spiritual experience; our stunted growth and continuing immaturity; our lack of love and devotion to God and to our fellow men; our spirit of grumbling and discontent; our quickness to criticise others, we shall marvel that God has called us to be co-labourers with Him. Only then shall we walk humbly with our God,

awed by His gracious patience and long-suffering forbearance.

"Acting justly" as Christ would, in each circumstance, and
so revealing Christ-likeness to others in all we do and how we
do it: "loving mercy" and yearning over the welfare of
suffering humanity around us, seeking by all means to bring
them to Christ; "walking humbly" before God who has
called us out of darkness into His marvellous light; this is
Holiness, revealing itself in service.

When Paul wrote to Titus, that God's grace teaches us
"... that denying ungodliness and worldly lusts, we should
live soberly, righteously and godly, in this present world;" he
went on to say that it is for this that Christ has redeemed us:
to "... purify unto Himself a peculiar people, zealous of
good works" (Titus 2:11–14) (AV). That is Christ's purpose
for us: to be "a peculiar people" zealous in His service. If we
allow Christ to work in our hearts a desire to be holy, then we
must expect to be considered peculiar – very peculiar! – by
all who live by other standards than God's.

The first of these three phrases: "denying ungodliness and
worldly lusts", can be considered as the negative aspect of
Holiness, the essential Biblical "do nots". Ungodliness
simply means leaving God out of our reckoning: acting as
though there were no God. Men by their own reasoning have
devised their own system of situational ethics, without
regard to God's laws or standards. The result is not unlike
what would happen if one filled a car with lemonade instead
of petrol, or if a team played a football match to their own set
of rules, without discussion with the opposing team. Chaos!

Though God created us, and therefore knows how we can
function best, and has provided us with a book of
instructions so that we can get the very best out of the life
that He has entrusted to us, we can choose to ignore Him, go
our own way and make up our own rules. That is
ungodliness. Furthermore, questioning the very existence of
God as Creator and Sustainer, as Saviour and King, as well
as questioning His relevance to our generation, and His right

to set the rules, and His authority to demand our obedience, is ungodliness.

"Worldly lusts" are those forces that govern, direct and control much of today's world. As we look around the nations of the world, we see people governed by a vast, egocentric attitude. Greed, selfishness and pride often overshadow what is popularly called "our better nature". The desire to dominate, to be popular, or simply to make a success, drives many onward, no matter what means are employed.

To deny worldly lusts is to say "No" to all that the world offers us that is not clearly in accord with God's character and standards, thereby showing the people among whom we live Whose we are, and Whom we serve.

The second of Paul's three phrases in his letter to Titus, to live "soberly, righteously and godly", can be considered as the positive aspect of Holiness; to say "Yes" to all that God shows us to be right and pleasing to Him. A public and visible declaration of intent to go God's way and to live self-controlled and upright lives is to say "Yes" to God's right to control my life according to His declared laws.

"Self-control" is one of the nine-fold fruit of the Holy Spirit. Those, who seek to live self-controlled and upright lives, will refuse to push themselves forward at another's expense. They will speak the truth with courtesy and restraint, and refrain from exaggeration that inflates the ego or avoids personal responsibility. They will refuse to deceive, or to use underhand means to gain more than is justly due, or to cheat in any form whatsoever to avoid just payment. They will behave with a quiet dignity that remains calm when falsely accused, and that refuses to get heated when slandered. They will maintain right standards even in the face of ridicule, and act justly even when by so doing an advantage is lost.

Instead of being dominated by the urgent question, "what can I get out of it?" a Christian should be steadily directed by the searching question, "what can I contribute to it?"

And so to the third phrase in Paul's letter to Titus: "to purify unto Himself a peculiar people, zealous of good works". Christ died to "redeem us from all wickedness", dealing with all the past by His death on Calvary; but also "to purify" us for service, enabling us by His risen life to live in the present in a manner pleasing to Him. We may be "zealous of good works", but for these good works to be acceptable to God, we must first know that we are being purified by His grace, in order that we may be His peculiar people.

* * *

To return to the story of Jonah. He knew that God wanted His people to be "set apart" and distinct from those about them, in order that they might serve Him acceptably. Jonah could see quite clearly that God's ways and the ways of the world around him were diametrically opposed.

But he couldn't face the consequences of that fact.

He had to learn that a Christian cannot say "No, Lord." Either we say, "Yes, Lord," or we simply say "No," refusing to acknowledge our Saviour as Lord. Once we say "Lord," we have to say "Yes," because His acknowledged lordship demands obedience.

Jonah knew that it was God's Voice that had said distinctly, "Arise, go to Nineveh," but he sought to argue. Yet even as he argued, the Holy Spirit showed him that he was wrong. He made him conscious of the fact that God did actually want him to go to Nineveh, to preach repentance, and probably to watch them turn to God and be forgiven!

Jonah loved God and wanted to serve Him – but he wanted to do it on his own terms. He lacked the basic essential of obedience – instant, unquestioning, unhesitating obedience – so God could not accept the proffered service. He must train Jonah first to obey Him.

Jonah did not submit easily to God's training!

"He rose up to flee from the face of the Lord," and

probably "put out a fleece" to prove to himself that he was actually doing what the Lord really meant him to do.

"If I find a ship about to sail, with an empty berth, for which I have sufficient money, I'll know that is really where God meant to send me," may have been his thoughts – though he would not have needed a ship at all to go to Nineveh, just a camel! And sure enough, there was the ship, with the berth, and he had just the right money! All circumstances lined up to prove that this was right – to go west, when God's plan was to send him east.

How easily we can think like that, if our motive to serve, though possibly born of a real heart-love for the Saviour and for mankind, is not actually governed by obedience. Are we willing to do the specific job that God wants us to do – that is, to carry the Candle to the place of His appointment?

"Yes, I'm willing to be God's candlestick, and that He should mould me to the shape and size He chooses.

"Yes, I'm willing to abide by the prescribed rules for carrying God's Candle, doing the job His way rather than my own.

"But I'm not sure if I am yet willing to let God choose the place of my service and that He alone should direct where I am to carry the Candle."

Is that our reaction?

When I came home from Africa in 1973, to share with my family in providing a home for our mother, she and I initially accepted an invitation to stay together at our Mission headquarters. We were both very happy and everyone was so good to us; yet after a few months I felt that it was wrong to remain there. It is not possible for the Mission to accept the care of the elderly parents of all our missionaries: headquarters simply is not big enough, has not sufficient staff, and lives at a pace impossible for the less able. We were, it seemed to me, presuming on their kindness.

So I looked round for employment. I felt that I needed a job that would both stretch me, and also give that elusive thing called "job satisfaction". Preferably, there should be a house provided with the job, with suitable living accommodation downstairs for my invalid mother. It would be good to have a sufficient salary to be able to pay someone to care for mother in the way she deserved, and to be a companion to her during the hours that I would be at work. I laid all that before the Lord, and mother and I prayed for His clear guidance.

Just the right job "came my way". The lady retiring from this job was seeking a Christian woman, with my qualifications, to take her place. It would be a five-year appointment initially, but with the expectancy of a fifteen-year tenure. There was a home, with absolutely the right ground-floor accommodation for mother. There would be a steady, secure and sufficient salary. This lady discussed it all with me, and urged me to apply for the appointment.

It was all so perfectly "right". Everything fitted exactly. It would be a great challenge, but I felt my previous experience would enable me to meet that challenge and to enjoy it. Even the timing was right – it would probably be fifteen years before the job became vacant again! "Yes, indeed," I reasoned, "God is good, and is obviously working on my behalf."

I resigned from our Mission and applied for the job.

God's ways are certainly mysterious at times, and this was one of those times. This turned out to be a case of what I call "negative guidance".

Every piece had fitted exactly into the jigsaw, or I would never have applied for the job, much in the same way as Jonah found a ship with an available berth. But God was at work behind the scenes for me, exactly as He had been for Jonah.

Once my resignation from the Mission and an application for this appointment were completed, my peace of heart left me. For a month, I was fretful and worried and anxious. I could settle to nothing. I could not sleep at nights. I dreaded going to the prayer meetings at headquarters, as I felt so ill at ease. Mother said I became irritable, almost unreasonable, even over small, inconsequential matters. By the end of the first month, my mother urged me to withdraw my application for the job, and to ask the Mission to defer my resignation.

"You are like a bear with a sore head," she said, "and I just can't stand any more of it. It is so obviously not God's will for you!"

I was startled by her words. I honestly wanted God's will, yet, uncertain as to the rightness of mother's reasoning, I hesitated. Was my nervousness possibly only fear of the unknown? Being a member of the Mission family had been my great security for twenty years. Was I simply afraid that I would not be able to manage the job, that it would prove too big for me? It would certainly demand even greater resourcefulness than all the tasks in Congo/Zaire, but the same God who undertook for me there could surely undertake for me now in this new venture. Yet I wondered, was mother right, that my loss of peace of mind signalled that I was venturing outside God's will for my life? So many voices clamoured to be heard.

"Helen, give it up!" mother pleaded with me. "Get back into WEC! You'll see I'm right."

I did. She was. Peace returned at once.

God had reached through to show me what *was* His will, by showing clearly what was *not* His will. To do this, He had allowed me to think that the second alternative might be His will – and everything had looked so right. But God's peace was withdrawn. "Negative guidance" if you like, but still guidance, and that guidance confirmed when His peace was restored.

Jonah received the same type of "negative guidance!"

Ship, berth, passage-money – all lined up – and he sailed away westwards, with his back to God's chosen destination, pleased that God had made everything fit so well. We have to learn that circumstantial guidance alone, even when everything seems to fit perfectly, is not a sufficiently sure proof that one is taking God's chosen pathway. This is particularly true when we know that there has been a moment of unwillingness on our part to do the particular job that God has appointed for us, and so an act of disobedience and a turning out of God's way have followed. "Then the Lord sent a great wind on the sea," we read in Jonah 1:4, "and such a violent storm arose that the ship threatened to break up." You could say, there was no peace! But Jonah was not yet ready to listen.

Others could see the storm, and the sailors were all afraid. Doubtless all the other passengers, and the sailors and passengers of any other ships in their vicinity, were also filled with fear by the overwhelming tempest. "But Jonah had gone below deck," we read, "where he lay down and fell into a deep sleep" (Jonah 1:5). What an incredible picture! Everyone suffering except, apparently, the cause of it all. Ultimately the owners and commercial traders, as well as the sailors and the other passengers, were all to lose enormously because of the tempestuous storm: "they threw the cargo into the sea, to lighten the ship" (Jonah 1:5).

God allowed the situation to arise in order to teach Jonah a lesson, a deep lesson: namely, that our service for God must be the result of obedience to the Voice of God. Jonah may well have intended to preach God's message in Tarshish. The intention to serve was there, but he sought to decide what would be best for God's cause! That did not, and does not, work.

True Christian service, as the expression of God's Holiness in an individual, must be motivated by obedience to God's will. There can be no room whatsoever for any "self" in the motivation, or it ceases to be holy.

Jonah was afraid for his "self" and self's image, if he were to obey God and go to Nineveh. Yet God knew that at heart Jonah did want to act in accordance with His will. So God cornered him, in a situation from which he could not flee, and Jonah capitulated to God's right to determine the terms of his service. "Pick me up and throw me into the sea," said Jonah, "and it will become calm" (Jonah 1:12), for he knew that he was the cause of the ferocious wind and wild storm. He was no coward. He was willing to accept the responsibility for the mess they were in, and showed the sailors what to do to restore calm. Nevertheless, the sailors tried with all their might to spare Jonah: they struggled to reach land in a desperate bid to overcome the storms but to no avail.

So we are told in Jonah 1:15: "Then they took Jonah and threw him overboard, and the raging sea grew calm".

Instant calm! God's peace prevailed.

Jonah, down in the fish's belly, realised that he had disobeyed God and, because of that, had lost God's peace in his heart. He acknowledged his fault and sought God's forgiveness, promising to obey His commands in the future; and God's Word tells us that "the Lord commanded the fish, and it vomited Jonah on to dry land" (Jonah 2:10).

It is very easy to offer God our service, as Jonah did, with certain reservations. I had told God that I was willing to be a candlestick and be moulded to His design and that I was willing to carry His Candle in the prescribed way. I had gone where He had appointed me; but now I was unwilling for Him to change the place and the nature of my service. I wanted to attach conditions to my service.

Service, to be acceptable to God, must be given as an unreserved act of total obedience to His will, with no part of "self" involved. There can be no qualifying conditions.

During my first furlough, I had the joy of seeing more patients accepting the Lord Jesus Christ as their Saviour during a six-month surgical residency in South Wales than I had seen during the four years of service at Nebobongo hospital. Ought I therefore to remain in medical service in the United Kingdom rather than return to the cross-cultural missionary situation at Nebobongo? The obvious flaws in such a simplistic evaluation of service hardly need attention drawn to them. If my ultimate objective was to see the largest possible number of people converted, then I would stay in the United Kingdom. If however my goal was to bring honour to God and glory to His name, I would obey Him and, answering His call, return to Nebobongo in Zaire.

The "flaws" in any system of evaluating the suitability of a candidate for a particular job are not always so obvious, and the enemy is intensely clever at muddling the issues.

It is, of course, right to seek to fit the right candle to the right candlestick, but this must not be in order to show off the workmanship of the candlestick! It must always be to seek what is best for the candle. Missionary service, as all other Christian service, if it is to be "holy and acceptable" to God, must flow from obedience, and not simply come from a desire to meet a need, however great that need may be. The fact that a missionary candidate appears to have the exact abilities needed to fulfil a particular task on the Mission Field, is, again, not sufficient evidence that that person is necessarily the one of God's choice.

It is obviously essential to try to know the state of the world we live in and to face the plight of millions of its inhabitants, in hunger and poverty; in ignorance or pain; under fanatical dictatorships or suffering from corrupt exploitation. World news on the media does move our hearts to realise the enormity of the task committed to us: "Go into *all* the world and preach the Good News to *all* creation" (Mark 16:15).

This knowledge, however, does not in itself constitute a call to service. We can be stirred and challenged and made to face up to our responsibilities by these means, but the call to Christian service must be in obedience to His Word and personal call.

When God says: "Arise and go to Nineveh..." it is not for us to consider whether Nineveh needs or deserves the message more than Tarshish, nor to reckon whether there is more probability of a response in Tarshish than in Nineveh. We are not asked whether Nineveh is in our programme or not, nor are we to debate as to the greater likelihood of finding a language teacher in Tarshish!

Can the clay pot argue with the Potter: "Why have You

not given me handles?"

Can a candlestick demand to be a saucepan, preferring to boil a potato to carrying the Candle into an unpropitious corner of the world?

* * *

Holiness will always show itself in obedient service.

Andrew Murray has two most useful comments that we might look at here. He says:

> It has sometimes been said that people might be better employed in working for God than attending Holiness Conventions. This is surely a misunderstanding. It was before the throne of the Thrice Holy One, and as he heard the seraphim sing of God's Holiness, that the prophet said: "Here am I, send me." As the missions of Isaiah, and Moses, and the Son, whom the Father sanctified and sent, had their origin in the revelation of God's Holiness, our missions will receive new power as they are more directly born out of the worship of God as the Holy One, and baptised into the Spirit of Holiness.

Secondly, he comments:

> Note the connection between "sanctified", and "meet for the Master's use". True Holiness is being possessed of God; true service is being used of God. How much service there is in which we are the chief agents, and ask God to help and to bless us! True service is being yielded up for the Master to use. Then the Holy Ghost is the Agent, and we are the instruments of His will. Such service is Holiness[1].

Inward Holiness is developed by the Holy Spirit in three "steps" – through hatred for sin, love for the Saviour and obedience to God. This Holiness of character is fore-ordained by God for all His adopted children, as Paul tells us in Ephesians 1:4-6:

> For he chose us in Him before the creation of the world to be *holy* and blameless in His sight. In love He predestined us to be adopted as His sons through Jesus Christ, in accordance with His pleasure and will – to the praise of His glorious grace, which He has freely given us in the One He loves.

Outward Holiness is revealed by the Holy Spirit in the life of the Christian, through the manifesting of the nine-fold fruit – love, joy, peace, patience, kindness, goodness, faithfulness, gentleness and self-control – in service to others. This Holiness of conduct is channelled into the good works that God has fore-ordained for each one of us: "For we are God's workmanship, created in Christ Jesus to do good works, which God prepared in advance for us to do" (Eph. 2:10). These good works are like the fragrance that filled the house when Mary broke the alabaster box, in order to pour out all the very costly ointment, to anoint the feet of our Lord Jesus Christ. He said that what she had done was "a good work, a beautiful thing".

Such service has to know the "must" of *obedience to love's compulsion*. All His life, Christ had this *must* upon Him.

As a twelve-year-old, in Jerusalem after the feast of the Passover, He said to His parents, "Didn't you know I had to be in My Father's house?" (Luke 2:49).

On His way from Jerusalem to Galilee, during His three years of ministry, it is said: "Now He (Jesus) had to go through Samaria" (John 4:4) – just to meet a needy woman, drawing water at the well.

As He went to the Garden of Gethsemane on that fateful last evening before Calvary, our Lord said to His disciples, "It is written: 'And He was numbered with the transgressors';

and I tell you that this must be fulfilled in Me" (Luke 22:37).

After the Resurrection, Jesus reminded His disciples of all He had taught them during His three years with them, and at the empty tomb, the angels said: "Remember how He told you, while He was still with you in Galilee: The Son of Man *must* be delivered into the hands of sinful men, be crucified and on the third day be raised again" (Luke 24:6,7) (my italics).

By His Holy Spirit, Christ challenges us with the same "must." "You will be told what you *must* do" (Acts 9:6) (my italics), God said to Paul, and a little later, God sent Ananias to Paul saying: "I will show him how much he *must* suffer for My name" (Acts 9:16) (my italics).

Paul and Barnabas taught the same message to their young converts in Galatia: "We *must* go through many hardships to enter the kingdom of God" (Acts 14:22) (my italics).

All our conduct and the whole outward service of our lives must be an expression of Holiness, that results from the *must* of obedience.

One could quote endlessly to illustrate how Holiness always reveals itself in service that reaches out to help others, as light pours out into a dark place.

All the records of revivals, be it in 1859 in Ulster, in 1904 in Wales, in the 1940's in Ruanda, in the 1950's in Zaire and in the Hebrides, tell stories of changed lives and active witness, the longing to serve born of a new Holiness of character that just has to share the Good News of Salvation with those still in darkness.

The important point to realise, however, is that, underlying all such illustrations and stories of selfless service to others, from church history and missionary chronicles, it is always *obedience* that motivates such service.

The person rendering that service may not necessarily look on it as an act of obedience, but rather as the overflow of love for God in gratitude for His overwhelming love for us. Nevertheless, it is the Holy Spirit in the believer's life who translates the need of one's heart to express this love into a life of obedience, poured out in service for others.

To clarify our understanding of the apparent overlapping of these four steps in the life of Holiness, may we look again at the illustration of the use of the four hoofs of a galloping horse? Each hoof is essential to the horse's progress. Each follows in steady rhythm, but the eye cannot observe the order in which they move. So is the ministry of the Holy Spirit in the heart of each believer, as He seeks to transform us into the likeness of Christ, by developing Holiness in our lives. Each step is essential, but we are not always conscious of the order in which one step has led on to the other.

What we *are* determines what we *do*. Jesus Himself made this abundantly clear in His great Sermon on the Mount. The first section of the beatitudes show us what we are to be by the grace of God. We are to be poor in spirit rather than proud, mournful for sin rather than indifferent, meek in submission rather than obstinate, hungry and thirsty for God's righteousness rather than for worldly success, merciful and compassionate rather than vindictive and judgmental, pure in heart rather than conformed to a socially acceptable low ethic, peacemakers rather than troublemakers, willing to be persecuted rather than to compromise.

Then the Lord showed us how this inner character of Holiness would reveal itself in outward conduct and service: "You are the light of the world ... let your light shine before men that they may see your good deeds and praise your Father in heaven" (Matt. 5:14–16).

Paul was inspired by the Holy Spirit to stress exactly the same order, when he wrote to the Philippians. He told them to be Christlike:

"... blameless and pure, children of God without fault in a crooked and depraved generation," before he enjoined them to "... shine like stars in the universe" (Phil. 2:12–15).

Our urgent prayer must always be: "Let us be thankful, and so worship God acceptably with reverence and awe. For our 'God is a consuming fire'" (Heb. 12:28,29).

Almighty God, in His terrible, awe-some, holy Majesty, is a "jealous" God (where jealousy means intolerance of unfaithfulness). He is jealous for my undivided love and loyalty. He is jealous that I should be holy. He has commanded me to have no graven image, no second cause, no ulterior motive, no selfish factor – but that I should love, obey and serve *Him* only.

You shall have no other gods before Me.

You shall not make for yourself an idol in the form of anything in heaven above or on the earth beneath or in the water below. You shall not bow down to them or worship them; for I, the Lord your God, am a jealous God ... showing love to a thousand generations of those who love Me and keep My commandments (Exod. 20:3–6).

This jealousy of God is *fire* – fire that can burn out sin and dross, fire that can melt and warm our hard and cold hearts, fire that can purify and harden our will to obey, and fire that can heat and shine through our lives in daily service to others.

For we do not preach ourselves, but Jesus Christ as Lord, and ourselves as your servants for Jesus's sake. For God, who said, "Let light shine out of darkness," made His light shine in our hearts to give us the light of the knowledge of the glory of God in the face of Christ.

But we have this treasure in jars of clay to show that this all-surpassing power is from God and not from us (2 Cor. 4:5–7).

May we be willing for all that God, our consuming fire, wants to do in our lives to make us acceptable candlesticks to carry Him, the Light of the world, wheresoever He wants to go: and may our prayer be:

Spirit of the living God, fall afresh on me.
Spirit of the living God, fall afresh on me.
  Break me – dealing with all the sin –
  Melt me – filling me with Your Divine love –
  Mould me – firing me to obedience to Your will –
  Use me – sending me out to serve You acceptably –
Spirit of the living God, fall afresh on me.

6

The attainable goal

By one sacrifice He has made perfect for ever those who are being made holy (Heb. 10:14).

The result of the single offering of the high priest is the attainment of perfection for believers. The emphasis must fall on the verb, "*He has perfected* (teteleioken)". This regards the action as already completed, in an anticipatory sense. In Himself, Christ gathered up all those whom He represents to share with them His perfection. The phrase "*those who are sanctified* (tous hagiazomenous)" is in the present continuous tense, "those who are constantly being sanctified".

Donald Guthrie[1].

The chief thought of the passage is: "He hath for ever perfected them that are being sanctified". The words in verse 10, "*In which Will we have been sanctified*," speak of our sanctification as an accomplished fact: we are saints, holy in Christ, in virtue of our real union with Him, and His holy life planted in the centre of our being. Here we are spoken of as "*being sanctified*". There is a process by which our new life in Christ has to master and to perfect Holiness through our whole outer being. But the progressive sanctification has its rest and its assurance in the *once* and *for ever* of Christ's work.

Andrew Murray[2].

6 The attainable goal

"Lord, show me . . ." is often the cry of our hearts, perhaps
most often in connection with another phrase ". . . the end
from the beginning".

Moses, brought face to face with God at the burning bush,
in the wilderness, after forty years of solitary shepherding, is
ordered to take off his sandals "for the place where you are
standing is holy ground".

Moses was deeply afraid. The ground could only be holy
because God was going to meet with him and speak to him,
and he hid his face.

God explained to Moses that He had seen the misery and
suffering of the Israelites in Egypt under the brutal
oppression of Pharaoh and his slave drivers, and that He,
God, was concerned on their behalf. "I have come down to
rescue them from the hands of the Egyptians and to bring
them up out of that land into a good and spacious land . . . So
now, go. I am sending *you* to Pharaoh to bring My people . . .
out of Egypt" (Exod. 3:8,10) (my italics).

When Moses began to remonstrate with God at the
impossibility of *his* being involved in such a programme,
God went on to say that he should go and tell the Israelites
that "I have promised to bring you up out of your misery in
Egypt into the land of the Canaanites . . . a land flowing with
milk and honey" (Exod. 3:17).

God gave Moses the promise of the *end* of the journey –
"into the land of the Canaanites . . . flowing with milk and
honey" – from the beginning of his call to service, before the
Israelites had even left Egypt. He did not, however, reveal to
Moses the details of the ten plagues that must first take place

before Pharaoh would let them so much as start on their journey. He did not explain to Moses the problems of water shortage and near famine conditions that the vast multitude would meet with before they reached Mount Horeb again. He did not warn Moses that the people would turn against him, seek to stone him, murmur and rebel over and over again, and finally refuse point blank to obey him or God whom he represented. He gave Moses no indication of the thirty-eight years of wandering in the wilderness, during which time almost every adult would die, including Aaron and Miriam, mostly because of their faithlessness and utter refusal to submit to authority.

Throughout those long years of rebellion, disobedience and unbelief, when God was angry with His people and swore that they should never enter into His rest (Heb. 3:7–19), Moses held on to the *vision* that God had given him at the outset, that they would ultimately enter into the land of the Canaanites "flowing with milk and honey".

The *vision* at the outset gave him the assurance that the goal *was* attainable, however long and arduous the process of "taking possession".

In May 1966, God gave *me* a vision – of a training college for national para-medical workers in a particular valley in north-east Zaire, where at that time there was nothing but elephant grass, brambles and briars.

I had returned to Zaire following the devastation of the civil war of 1964, to face, with our Christian family, the tremendous challenge of reconstruction. After three months of being immersed in the needs of thousands of school children without schools, equipment or staff; the needs of tens of thousands of refugees without food, shelter or any means of starting life again; the needs of over one million people for a meaningful medical service, where there were practically no buildings, no equipment and no satisfactorily qualified staff, I found it was not easy to decide on priorities.

Why were we back in Zaire? What were we meant to be doing, individually and as a group?

Dr Becker, veteran missionary doctor of the Africa Inland Mission, had already made his decision. All interested missionary societies and church congregations should create a new medical team which together should build one good central hospital for the vast region, where the care given to Africans in body, soul and spirit would be of the highest possible standard.

Would I join him?

We discussed the project... and slowly an overall plan began to form itself in our hearts and minds – hospital, outpatients, training school; regional hospitals and rural dispensaries; flying doctor service linking all together; central pharmacy...

Throughout our discussions, my mind kept flicking back to the need of a training school... Already I was mentally listing the subjects to be taught, methods of combining theoretical with practical training, report sheets and Government liaison. I was picturing classrooms and laboratory, nursing arts' demonstration room, library, offices and record filing. I was visualising dining hall and dormitories, uniforms and entrance exams.

I was excited! I could see graduates serving all over the vast north-eastern region of Zaire, as skilled medical evangelists... and I set about selling my "vision" to others who would be involved in its implementation.

Then there was the long journey to Kinshasa, the Government capital of the country, to secure "their rubber stamp on our blue prints!" This involved three weeks of foot-slogging and dogged perseverance, to seek out the right people who would not only be interested in our suggested programme but who would have sufficient authority to give us the green light to put it into practice.

Eventually, after innumerable set-backs and discouragements, I reached Dr Trieste's office. He arrived ten minutes late for our appointment, and transfixed me with sharp, piercing eyes.

"What do you want?" he demanded brusquely.

"Sympathy!" I blurted out, in my limited French.

Taken aback, he paused – and then actually smiled!

I leapt in and outlined hurriedly the whole desperate situation in the war-torn north-east, and the plan forming in our minds to meet the vast medical needs of the people.

He listened, at first idly, doodling on his blotting paper, then more intently, eventually being caught up by my enthusiasm into jotting down notes. *Then* things started to happen.

"OK. How concrete are your plans? Have you a time-table for achieving all this? Building plans? Curricula?"

I gulped – gazed – and pledged anything he wanted!

"Give me the use of a typewriter, paper, carbons and a pen," I said, "and I'll produce all you want."

"Go ahead then – use my desk," he generously offered. "I've a meeting with the Minister in ten minutes. I'll tell him that I want to see him again tomorrow with your proposals."

He left and I started work, from 10a.m. through to almost midnight. I drew plans of proposed buildings; I worked out time-tables for a four-year course both for students and for staff; I made out a decidedly optimistic budget with no suggestions as to where the funds would come from... By midnight I had left the completed file, in triplicate, on Dr Trieste's desk, drawn up as an eight-year project to establish the training school.

Two weeks later, permission was granted to go ahead with the scheme[3].

So our vision was born.

Like Moses at the burning bush, I felt that I stood on holy ground, and I was awed by the enormous task God had committed to my care; but I was absolutely sure that it was God's voice I had heard and that it was His plan, not my own, and that therefore He would bring it to pass. It was an attainable goal, because God had revealed it.

I had to go back and share the vision with the people who would have to turn it into practical reality with me. Like Moses, I received a less-than-enthusiastic welcome. Everyone could see the problems, the hurdles, the impossibilities. "Who will do the initial work?" some of the sceptics queried.

"The first group of students," I dared to reply.

"Impossible!" everyone expostulated. "They'll never co-operate."

And so on. There was no money, no qualified overseer, no transport, no equipment, no . . . and the list went on and on. But God had given a Vision.

For a week, day after day, I gazed down the mountainside on to the four to five acres of land that had been designated for the College. I prayed and asked God to show me exactly what He wanted, so that I could "make everything according to the pattern shown" me on the mountain (Heb. 8:5). I walked over the area, pushing my way through the tall grass, slithering in the mud, imagining each part of the future Nurses' Training School, trying to see into the future.

Then the first students arrived . . . and the testing started.

God had not told me of all the troubles that would erupt in the ensuing eight years – trade union problems relating to the workmen; discipline problems among the students; problems with the local Government who were unwilling to accept a white director in the days of black leadership; frequent problems with regard to needed supplies – lack of building material and means of transportation.

God did not warn me that the word given by one group of administrators in 1966 was not binding on a future group of administrators in 1970: I had nothing in writing. God did not open my eyes to realise that as numbers grew, I would not be able to carry the load alone as in the past, and that new team members would not be willing to work at my pace. God did not share with me that my closest friend and colleague would have to leave, nor that my own health would crack under the strain before the job was finished.

A visitor today can see the college with its dormitories and classrooms, its dining hall and facilities for seventy-two students; the lists of those who have graduated and are now in full-time church service in distant rural dispensaries and hospitals; and the office with its student files and records of Government approval.

The goal has been achieved.

God, who gave us the vision, enabled us to work it out – by hard-slogging perseverance in determined obedience and unremitting service. The work was not always enjoyable: there were many tears shed in the process. The way ahead was not always clear: there were times of doubt and deep uncertainty. Yet the witness to God's unfailing goodness in the fulfilment of His purpose, despite the failings and human frailty of His servant, took over one hundred pages to record![3]

*   *   *

However, that is the fulfilment of a fairly short-term calling. What about our ultimate vision, not just for some specific task during our earthly pilgrimage, but for all eternity? "Without Holiness no one will see the Lord" (Heb. 12:14).

My goal is certainly to "see the Lord". Above all else, I long to see Him, in all His beauty and majesty. Therefore I want to know, with utter certainty, that "Holiness" is attainable.

"Dear friends," said the apostle John, "now we are children of God, and what we will be has not yet been made known. But we know that when He appears, we shall be like Him, for we shall see Him as He is. Everyone who has this hope in Him purifies himself, just as He is pure" (1 John 3:2,3).

My hope is undoubtedly to see Him when He appears, and so I should be willing to go to all lengths to "purify myself" even as He is pure.

Is it possible to purify oneself? Could it be that God has set a standard for us, but not given us the power to achieve it? God forbid! That would simply be to mock us, and would be contrary to His very nature. It is God Himself who has said that He wants to make us holy, and certainly He will provide us with the means to that end.

In his book on the history and message of the Keswick Convention, Dr Steven Barabas asks some rhetorical questions like these: "Does God make demands on human beings that they cannot fulfil? Does He expect of them conduct beyond their reach? Are His requirements unreasonable? Is Christianity merely a religion of lofty ideals – ideals to be striven for, but without any hope of attaining them? In the divine programme for the Church, are Christians to be like Tantalus, who was in water up to his neck, yet could never quench his burning thirst, and who saw trees laden with fruit waving their branches directly over his head, yet could never reach them to satisfy his gnawing hunger; or like Sisyphus who had to roll a huge stone up a steep mountainside, and found that whenever he partially succeeded, the stone always rolled down again?"

But then he goes on to state categorically: "There is no suggestion anywhere in Scripture that God's requirements of Christians are unattainable, or that He overlooks and condones their failure to meet them. Nothing is more clear than that God expects a consistent, and not merely a spasmodic and intermittent, walk in the Spirit, with all that connotes of unbroken fellowship with Him, victory over sin, and steady growth in Christ-likeness. God's requirements cannot be greater than His enablements. If they were, man would be mocked"[4].

Paul, while disclaiming attainment, yet clearly implies that the goal is attainable, when he says: "I press on to take hold of that for which Christ Jesus took hold of me. Brothers, I do not consider myself yet to have taken hold of it. But one thing I do: Forgetting what is behind and straining towards what is ahead, I press on towards the goal..." (Phil. 3:12–14). And this goal is the attainment of personal Holiness by the Holy Spirit's activity in the heart of every believer.

Dr Andrew Bonar, in his biography of Robert Murray

M'Cheyne, quotes these words: "I am persuaded that I shall obtain the highest amount of present happiness, I shall do most for God's glory and the good of man, and I shall have the fullest reward in eternity, by (a) maintaining a conscience always washed in Christ's blood, by (b) being filled with the Holy Spirit at all times, and by (c) *attaining* the most entire likeness to Christ in mind, will and heart, that it is possible for a redeemed sinner to attain in this world. *The greatest need of those around me is my personal Holiness*"[5]. M'Cheyne was not here speaking only of his own greatest need but also of the need of those around him.

Do I believe that the greatest need of those around me is my personal Holiness?

I should not only long to "see the Lord" myself when He returns in glory, but I should also long that countless others will be there to see Him too. If I am to help those others to "purify themselves" that they may "see the Lord", my own mirror must be clean. Isn't that what Murray M'Cheyne is saying?

On the last page of that biography, Andrew Bonar asks this question: "Are we never afraid that the cries of souls whom we have betrayed to perdition *through our want of personal Holiness* and our defective preaching of Christ crucified, may ring in our ears for ever?"

This is a frightening thought, but surely should stir us to greater determination to "attain the goal" that God has set us.

Our Lord says to us: "If anyone causes one of these little ones who believe in me to sin, it would be better for him to have a large millstone hung around his neck and to be drowned in the depths of the sea." What powerful words from the tender, compassionate Saviour!

Then He goes on to underline, even more dramatically, the sheer horror of being a stumbling block in the path of another: "Woe to the world because of the things that cause people to sin! Such things must come, but woe to the man through whom they come!" (Matt. 18:6,7).

The Lord Jesus Christ is saying as clearly as it can be said that enormous responsibility is placed on every Christian towards those around him, especially towards children, who watch and copy every act and word. Not only must I seek personal Holiness in my life for my own well-being and eternal happiness, but even more so for the sake of those who "follow me", copying my example, that they also may be holy as He commanded. There must be nothing, absolutely nothing, in my daily conduct that, copied by another, could lead that one into unholiness.

In bitter self-recrimination, an officer at a youth camp was once heard to cry out in heart anguish, "God, forgive me! God, forgive me!" when he heard of a young man who committed suicide as an alcoholic. Many years before, that young alcoholic had been a teenager at camp where the older man was an officer. One evening, he, with a group of older campers, had gone to an inn and had a drink together, before noticing that the youngster was amongst them.

"I introduced him to his first taste of strong drink," the heart-broken man sobbed, "and now he is dead, a helpless alcoholic – God, forgive me!"

Paul underscores so clearly our Lord's teaching on this matter. He weighed up every action and practice in his life to be sure that he would never stumble another. "Everything is permissible for me," he said, "but not everything is beneficial, not everything is constructive." (1 Cor. 6:12; 10:23). He was thinking of the benefit to others, who might be watching his life as an example to follow. He went to great lengths to be sure that he was not a stumbling block to another Christian, by what he did, or wore, or ate, be the other Jew or Gentile.

"So whether you eat or drink or whatever you do, do it all for the glory of God," Paul wrote to the Corinthians. "Do not cause anyone to stumble, whether Jews, Greeks or the Church of God – even as I try to please everybody in every way. For I am not seeking my own good but the good of many, so that they may be saved. Follow my example, as I follow the example of Christ" (1 Cor. 10:31–11:1).

How then can we attain to this living experience of personal Holiness?

Firstly, we have seen that there must be a radical break with sin, a deliberate forsaking of the world and its ways.

Secondly, the true love of God will show itself in the life of each Christian, by a self-giving service, and a compassionate caring for those among whom we live. This will be the obvious fruit by which holy Christians will be known.

Thirdly, obedience will be given gladly to every known commandment of God, as the way by which we manifest our love for Christ. "When our lives are separated from the world and unto Christ in obedience," said Hugh Morgan, "then we give evidence of our love to Christ, for we do those things which please Him"[6]. The more we hate sin and love God, so much the more we shall strive by obedience to be conformed to the image of God's Son.

Fourthly, as Morgan goes on to say: "Holiness is the most effective way of influencing unconverted people and creating within them a willingness to listen to the preaching of the Gospel. Or, to put it negatively, a lack of personal Holiness is an excellent way of keeping needy souls from Christ."

These four "steps" towards the attainment of personal Holiness may involve, indeed almost certainly will demand, brokenness. Do you remember the weapons that were in the hands of the soldiers of Gideon's army? We are told in Judges 7 that when God had whittled down their numbers to a mere three hundred, He gave Gideon a strategy by which he could overcome the enemy's thousands. "Dividing the three hundred men into three companies," we read, "he placed trumpets and empty jars in the hands of all of them, with torches inside" (Judg. 7:16).

With this strange armour and complete lack of conventional weapons, the troops were told to split up and move forward under cover of dark in total silence. They were to keep their eyes on their leader, Gideon, and do exactly as he did.

Suddenly the stillness of the night was shattered as first Gideon, and then immediately the three hundred others, blew their trumpets. The sleeping enemy woke to the realisation that they were surrounded, possibly by three hundred companies of foot soldiers, each company's trumpeter blasting their battle cry!

Before they had time to think coherently, another crashing cacophony echoed to and fro from hillside to hillside around the campsite, as the three hundred empty jars were jettisoned and smashed on the ground. Each soldier waved aloft his smouldering flax, held in his left hand, and the torches blazed into flaming brands in the cold night air, lighting up the whole valley beneath them. Trumpeting defiantly, the soldiers charged forward into the terrified Midianite army, which fled in total disarray.

God gave the Israelites a resounding victory, as they broke the clay jars that covered the torches in obedience to His Word. At the given moment, the light streamed forth and led them forward to a mighty triumph.

Are we reminded again of Mary, who broke the alabaster jar, in order to pour the very expensive ointment on the head of the Lord Jesus Christ, "to prepare Him for His burial"? The released fragrance of the ointment filled the whole house where they sat. Mary had sought to show Christ the depth of her devotion, and nothing else would do but the best – and all the best. So the jar that she held had to be smashed to release the perfume (Mark 14:3–9).

When our Lord took the young lad's picnic lunch into His hands and blessed it, we are told in Mark 6:39–43, that He had to break the loaves before He could feed the vast multitude sitting on the grassy mountainside.

In Mark 14:12,22, we read, "On the first day of the Feast of Unleavened Bread, when it was customary to sacrifice the Passover Lamb... Jesus took bread, gave thanks and broke it, and gave it to His disciples, saying, 'Take it; this is My body.'"

The holy Lamb of God went from that feast to Calvary,

where His body was nailed to the tree, and broken for me and for you. His holy life was poured out in that great sacrifice in order that you and I might exchange our sinfulness for His Holiness. "God made him [Jesus] who had no sin to be sin for us, so that in Him we might become the righteousness of God" (2 Cor. 5:21).

The servant cannot be greater than the master. If I would serve Christ and my fellow men, as He served me, I must be willing – indeed, I must expect – to be broken to release the "fragrance of the knowledge of Him" (2 Cor. 2:14). We do not need to fear the breaking, because we are held in His nail-pierced hands, but He cannot feed others through us if we resist the breaking.

The God who commands also enables. He declares that we are to be holy *because* He is willing and able to make us holy. He who will break us from all unholiness and pride was first broken Himself on Calvary, that He might fill us with all Holiness and humility.

In 1 Corinthians 1:2, Paul writes: "To those made *holy* in Christ Jesus, and called to be holy" (my italics).

These three words, "Holy in Christ", are the title of a very wonderful book written in the last century by Andrew Murray, in which he brings together the two thoughts, (a) that we are to be *holy*, and (b) that God supplies the means to that end, *in Christ*.

Holy! [he writes] the word which reveals the purpose with which God from eternity thought of man, and tells what man's highest glory in the coming eternity is to be; to be partakers of His Holiness.

In Christ! the word in which all the wisdom and love of God are unveiled! The Father giving His Son to be one with us; the Son dying on the Cross to make us one with Himself; the Holy Spirit dwelling in us to establish and maintain that union.

Holy in Christ! . . . the two thoughts combined. Here is God's provision for our Holiness and His response to our question, "How can I be holy?" *In Christ* is the bridge that crosses the gulf between God and man[7].

God has provided all the means for the realisation of true personal Holiness, for has He not said: "I am the Lord who brought you up out of Egypt to be your God; therefore be holy because I am holy" (Lev. 11:45). "Keep My decrees and follow them. *I am the Lord who makes you holy*" (Lev. 20:8) (my italics).

This is the thought in the introductory quotations to this chapter, "... we *have been made holy* through the sacrifice of the body of Jesus Christ once for all... because by one sacrifice He has made perfect for ever those who are *being made holy*" (Heb. 10:10,14).

Here we have the fact stated that we "have been made holy" by the sacrifice of our Lord. When we feel discouraged, these are words to grasp and remember. It is God at work in us which ultimately leads to that moment for which we strive, and we can rest assured that with Him "nothing is impossible". Our responsibility, by faith, is to obey God's every known command so that we are "being made holy" in experience.

As I recognise that the greatest need both for myself and for all those around me is my personal Holiness, so I shall allow God full possession of my life, that I may be an empty, cleansed vessel, that He can fill to overflowing with Himself: "We have this treasure in jars of clay to show that this all-surpassing power is from God and not from us" (2 Cor. 4:7).

Epilogue

Christ is all (Col. 3:11).

The words of the text which heads this page are few, short and soon spoken; but they contain great things.

These three words are the essence and substance of Christianity. If our hearts can really go along with them, it is well with our souls. If not, we may be sure we have much yet to learn.

Christ is the mainspring both of doctrinal and practical Christianity. A right knowledge of Christ is essential to a right knowledge of sanctification as well as justification. He that follows after Holiness will make no progress unless he gives to Christ His rightful place.

J. C. Ryle[1].

Epilogue

God, who has promised to "make us holy", is faithful, and He cannot break His word. Moreover He has given us a sign to remind us of His covenant relationship with us, which can never be broken:

And God said, "This is the sign of the covenant I am making between Me and you and every living creature with you, a covenant for all generations to come: I have set My *rainbow* in the clouds, and it will be the sign of the covenant between Me and the earth. Whenever I bring clouds over the earth and the rainbow appears in the clouds, I will remember my covenant between Me and you and all living creatures of every kind... I will see it and remember the everlasting covenant" (Gen. 9:12–16) (my italics).

Ezekiel saw the Lord, high and lifted up, sitting on a throne of sapphire, "a figure like that of a man... full of fire... and brilliant light surrounded Him." Then Ezekiel records: "Like the appearance of a *rainbow* in the clouds on a rainy day, so was the radiance around Him. This was the appearance of the likeness of the *glory* of the *Lord*" (Ezek. 1:26–28) (my italics).

John, an exile on the island of Patmos, lifted up his eyes to heaven and also saw the Lord, sitting on a throne, and said: "And the One who sat there had the appearance of jasper and carnelian. A *rainbow*, resembling an emerald, encircled the throne" (Rev. 4:3) (my italics).

* * *

It was a dull and overcast morning as we set out from Kampala on the long drive home to Nyankunde in Zaire. The Landrover and trailer were packed to capacity with urgently needed supplies for hospital and missionaries. I was fearful lest all the paper work might not be in order and that we might have trouble at the customs.

My father and step-mother were accompanying us, their first visit to our country; and again, I found myself uneasy, lest the border guards refuse to recognise their visas, or the unrest in the national army flare up into open rebellion during the next two weeks, when they were with us.

I had planned that we should break our journey for lunch at the Murchison Falls, and so reach the Uganda/Zaire border at about four in the afternoon, when we knew from past experience there was least likelihood of delay, as the shifts changed over before five, and the officials would want us to get away quickly.

As we turned off the main road, towards the Falls, grey clouds filled the sky and a light rain began to fall. I was disappointed, for I had wanted my parents and my two African colleagues to see the magnificence of the Falls in all their splendour – and that needed clear sunshine.

We had a picnic lunch, and wandered across the open park-land towards the roaring thunder of the mighty river as it crashed ceaselessly downwards in an enormous cascade into a seething cauldron of spray. Leaning against the somewhat rickety fence, we watched, fascinated. We tried to follow the course of the water, but the speed of incessant movement mesmerised us. I felt as though each drop of water represented the people of our world, rushing on to an inevitable end, and I felt helpless and inadequate.

The thunder was deafening. Benjamin and Basuana, my African friends, watched, spellbound. They had never conceived of anything so awesome and powerful. In the dull, overcast light, it was a frightening scene of almost inconceivable grandeur.

Suddenly, there was a break in the clouds. The sun shone

through... and there before us, in the ever-rising spray, was a complete and dazzling rainbow.

It was incomparably beautiful. It was so perfect that we felt our breath caught in a never-to-be-forgotten moment of absolute stillness...

Awed, Basuana summed up in three words our sense of wonder at the majesty and overwhelming loveliness of the moment:

"Isn't God wonderful?"

As one traces God's wonderful plan of salvation and His purpose for every one of His children, truly all one can say is: "Isn't God wonderful?" Indeed, He is. And not only wonderful, but also:

"Glorious in Holiness."

Who among the gods is like You, O Lord?
Who is like You –
 majestic in Holiness,
 awesome in glory,
 working wonders? (Exod. 15:11) (my italics).

Notes to Sources

Prologue

1. *Holiness* by Bishop J. C. Ryle, published by Evangelical Press
2. Ibid: in the foreword by Dr J. I. Packer to the new 1979 edition – a statement made by Bishop F. J. Chavasse of Bishop J. C. Ryle

Chapter 1

1. *The Holiest of All* by Revd Andrew Murray, published by Marshall, Morgan and Scott
2. "Dr G. Campbell Morgan Memorial Lecture for 1955" given by Professor R. A. Finlayson at Westminster Chapel, London
3. Booklets by Mr Ted Hegre to illustrate the Cross in the life of the believer, obtainable from Bethany Fellowship, 6820 Auto Club Road, Minneapolis, Minnesota 55438 USA
4. *The Epistles of John* by John Stott, published by IVP

Chapter 2

1. *Sin and Temptation* by John Owen, published by Pickering and Inglis, 1983
2. *Holiness* by Bishop J. C. Ryle, published by Evangelical Press

3. *C. T. Studd* by Norman Grubb, published by Lutterworth Press
4. *After C. T. Studd* by Norman Grubb, published by Lutterworth Press
5. *This is That,* published by Christian Literature Crusade, 1954
6. *The Fifty-nine Revival* by Ian R. K. Paisley
7. *The Welsh Revival of 1904* by Eifion Evans
8. *W. P. Nicholson, Flame for God in Ulster* by S. W. Murray
9. *Revival in Lisburn* by Rev J. N. Spence
10. *Duncan Campbell, A Biography* by Andrew Woolsey, published by Hodder & Stoughton
11. *Sin and Temptation* by John Owen, introduction by Dr J. I. Packer. Reprinted by Pickering and Inglis, 1983

Chapter 3

1. *On Loving God* by Bernard of Clairvaux, published by Pickering and Inglis
2. *The Pursuit of God* by A. W. Tozer, published by Oliphants
3. *Song of Love* by Richard Rolle de Hampole (1290–1349), edited and translated by George C. Heseltine – Longmans, Green and Co. Reprinted in the *Anthology of Devotional Literature*
4. *A Treatise on Religious Affections* by Jonathan Edwards (1703–1778), reprinted in the *Anthology of Devotional Literature*
5. "From heaven You came" by G. Kendrick, from *Thankyou music* 1984; in *The Servant King* Songs of Fellowship, a Kingsway Publication
6. *Duncan Campbell, A Biography* by Andrew Woolsey, published by Hodder & Stoughton

Chapter 4

1. *My Utmost for His Highest* (readings for July 19th and September 22nd) by Oswald Chambers, published by Marshall, Morgan and Scott
2. *Royal Commandments* (prefatory note and p14, second day) by Frances Ridley Havergal, published 1886
3. *If* by Amy Carmichael (Dohnavur Fellowship), published by London SPCK, 1963
4. *Christian Maturity* by James Philip, published by IVP, 1973

Chapter 5

1. *Holy in Christ* (reading for the twenty-seventh day) by Revd Andrew Murray
2. *New Bible Commentary*; IVP production
3. *My Utmost for His Highest* (reading for January 17th) by Oswald Chambers, published by Oswald Chambers Publications Association and Marshall, Morgan and Scott

Chapter 6

1. *Hebrews* by Donald Guthrie, one of the Tyndale New Testament Commentaries, published by IVP
2. *The Holiest of All* by Revd Andrew Murray, published by Marshall, Morgan and Scott
3. *He Gave Us a Valley* by H. M. Roseveare, published by IVP
4. *So Great Salvation, The History and Message of the Keswick Convention* by Dr Steven Barabas, published by Marshall, Morgan and Scott
5. *Robert Murray M'Cheyne* by Andrew Bonar, published by the Banner of Truth Trust

6. *The Holiness of God and His People* by Hugh D. Morgan, published by the Evangelical Press of Wales
7. *Holy in Christ* by Revd Andrew Murray

Epilogue

1. *Holiness* by Bishop J. C. Ryle, published by Evangelical Press